I0647071

The Red Roof
and
Other Stories

Written by Tie Ning

New Classic Press

2024

NEW CLASSIC PRESS

Published by New Classic Press (UK) ★
5th Floor, 99 Mansell Street, London, E1 8AX, UK,
Great Britain ★ Established in the year 2008 ★
Seeking business opportunities worldwide

The Red Roof and Other Stories

Written by Tie Ning
Translated by Anthony Rash
Original Edition © Changjiang Children's Press (Group) Co., Ltd, 2021
This English Edition Published in the United Kingdom of Great Britain
and Northern Ireland
by New Classic Press Limited in 2024

All rights reserved

ISBN 978-1-917143-13-4

First printed in the United Kingdom of Great Britain and Northern Ireland

10 9 8 7 6 5 4 3 2 1

DESIGNED BY SRA BERKS

Without limiting the rights under copyright reserved above, no part of
this publication may be reproduced, stored in or introduced into a retrieval
system, or transmitted, in any form or by any means (electronic, mechanical,
photocopying, recording, or otherwise), without the prior written
permission of both the copyright owner and the above publisher of this
book.

The publisher's policy is to use paper manufactured from sustainable forests.

B&R Book Program

CONTENTS

1 Hope 001

2 A Thousand Pieces of Candy Wrappers 015

3 Kite Fairy...025

4 Communicating with Strangers.........................037

5 The Faint Afterglow..............................050

6 Gold and Diamonds 069

7 A Country Party in Stevenson County.................083

8 The Red Roof....................................097

Writer's Album 276

Writer's Handwriting 293

1

Hope

I had two pet peeves: the first was dishonesty, and the other, was rainy weather.

In June, it used to rain so much that you couldn't go out during class breaks unless you had raincoats. Those lucky few with rain gear frolicked in the rain, getting more and more excited as the harder it poured. Meanwhile, the rest of us without raincoats were stuck indoors in the classroom. Wah-la-wah, wah-la-wah! It was as if the rain had transformed our third-grade classroom into a frog-filled pond. We could play "Catch the Goat" with our hands, yet our legs and feet were left idle, having nothing to do. That was when I was totally into the game rubber band skipping and I already mastered the "big lift" jump. Even Uncle Zhang, our school's janitor, had got to know that I was almost catching up with Zhao Xiaoyun, the reigning queen of the game and also my deskmate.

Then one day, my mum returned from work and handed me a flat paper box. Inside was a new raincoat, transparent and light green! I wasted no time putting it on. But wait! This raincoat had two sleeves! And it was unlike Zhao Xiaoyun's cloak-style one! Zhao's cloak kept her hands confined inside only. With this raincoat, things could be very different. Whether it rained or not, I had full freedom. If I wanted to put my arm around Zhao Xiaoyun's shoulder, I could easily lift my arm. If she tried the same, it wouldn't be so straightforward for her. I pondered this as I wandered around the house, wearing my rain hat, swishing my sleeves, and rustling my raincoat. It wasn't until my mum yelled, "Leilei, are you crazy? Do you want to get prickly heat?" that I took off the raincoat. My shirt was damp with sweat, and I felt a chill.

The following day, I hurried to school and shared with Zhao Xiaoyun about my treasure stored in the flat box. She exclaimed with joy, "Had it rained today, I would have witnessed you donning it." I had intended to outshine her "cloak style" raincoat, but her genuine happiness for me left me feeling somewhat bashful. Yet, I couldn't shake off the thought that perhaps it was because she hadn't yet actually seen it. When the rain poured down and we each donned our raincoats, it would be hard to tell if she would still be pleased for me!

I started to anticipate rainy days eagerly. However, for many consecutive days, the sky remained clear blue during the day and starlit at night. My raincoat rested silently in its box, which in turn was tucked away in the closet. Every day on my way home from school, I wondered: How could there be clouds under the scorching sun? Why did the weather forecast always predict "sunny" days when I had a raincoat to wear? I used to dislike rainy days because I didn't have a raincoat, but now, things had changed.

One day, as I was about to arrived at home, the leaves of the poplar trees on the roadside suddenly rustled, as if they were chuckling. There was no need to ask – it was the wind. A short while later, a few thick clouds drifted over, casting a shadow over the sun. The weather changed rapidly. While pedestrians on the road hastened their pace, I slowed down, imagining how wonderful it would be to feel the first raindrops on my head! As if on cue, accompanied by distant rumbles of thunder, a few droplets landed on my head. I reached out, and two raindrops fell onto my hand. It felt like my wish had been granted, and with excitement, I glanced up, swung my schoolbag around, and strode through the door of the apartment building.

"Mum!" I screamed as I ran into the kitchen.

"Leilei, you come back at the right time. Dry your hair and get ready for the English

TV lecture!"

"But ... there is still half an hour left," I muttered, thinking why Mum didn't just look out of the window.

"Then take a break and relax your mind." After that, I heard a sizzling sound. It was Mum putting garlic scapes into the boiling oil.

"I'm not tired today, not even a bit. Mum, let me get you some soy sauce, huh?" I begged.

"Look, I have bought it after work myself." Mum smiled at me as if she had guessed what I intended to.

"But ... don't we have to stew the meat? You need to put lots and lots of soy sauce in the stew." I said while darting my eyes out the window, worrying that the rain would stop.

"What's wrong with you today? When did I say anything about stewing the meat?" Mum braised rice and turned to me.

"You didn't, but Dad did." I blushed as soon as the words came out of my mouth. Because it was a lie. I hadn't met Dad, not to mention that Dad told me about the stew thing.

"Really?" mum asked.

I fell silent and avoided looking at Mum, not wanting her to see my flushed face. Hastily, I turned to gaze at the dish rack filled with bottles and jars, realizing there was little chance of going out to buy anything. Glancing at the alarm clock in the living room—6:20 pm—I resigned myself to turning on the TV and quietly listening to the English lecture.

After dinner, the rain continued to fall, pitter-pattering and tick-tocking against the glass windows as if it were drumming a beat, enticing me to step outside. I dashed to the window and peered down the street. While doing so, I couldn't help but ponder: If it rains all day today, will it also rain tomorrow? Perhaps it would be wiser to save this excitement for tomorrow.

Surprisingly, the rain ceased just as I had anticipated. Suddenly, all was quiet outside. I opened the window, letting in fresh air infused with an earthy scent. In the glow of the streetlight, the rain-washed road shimmered like a sheet of polished glass; the poplar trees lining the street appeared adorned with pearls and agates. I couldn't help but imagine how beautiful the rain would look on my light green raincoat. It would surely surpass the splendor of pearls and agates. With excitement, I flung myself into bed, eagerly anticipating what would unfold when the rain fell on my raincoat the next day.

The next morning, I woke up and found

the outside world disappointingly silent. However, I refused to let it dampen my spirits. I chose to stay positive and put thoughts of rain out of my mind. To my surprise, as I walked down the street with my backpack, a few drops of water landed on my head. Initially, I assumed they had dripped from the trees. It wasn't until I looked up and moved away from the trees that I realized the sweet drops on my lips were indeed raindrops. My heart raced with excitement. I hurried home in a few quick strides, dashed to the closet, and grabbed my raincoat. Excitedly, I exclaimed to my mum, "Mum, it's raining! Rain again!"

Mum smiled at me with a tilt of her head. She helped me fasten my buttons and put on my hat. I kept my head held up and carefully ran downstairs.

As I strolled down the street, donning my

two transparent green sleeves, I couldn't shake the feeling of being watched by countless envious eyes. Even the raindrops appeared to target my raincoat exclusively, bouncing energetically on my head and shoulders— pitter-patter, pitter-patter—as if dancing around me. How delightful it would be if Zhao Xiaoyun happened to come over by at that moment!

Zhao Xiaoyun was nowhere to be seen on the street, while the doorkeeper, Uncle Zhang, hurriedly escorted a girl who appeared to be not much older than me. I couldn't help but wonder why they weren't wearing raincoats or carrying umbrellas. What was even more peculiar was that Uncle Zhang was only wearing a vest. Wasn't he feeling cold? As I approached, I noticed that his blue uniform was wrapped around a violin case, and the girl was holding the case tightly against her chest. For some inexplicable reason, a strange notion crossed my mind – Uncle Zhang would be better off not seeing me in my raincoat. Therefore, I quickly hid in a doorway at the side of the road.

Finally, Uncle Zhang came by. With a sigh of relief, I slipped out of the doorway. I reassumed my imagined comparison of raincoats with Zhao Xiaoyun. The raindrops continued to bounce on my shoulders, but their sound no longer felt as melodious as before. It was as if they were now mocking at and taunting someone—could they be gossiping about my sneaky behavior just moments ago? I tried to push the thought aside, but the harder I tried, the louder the raindrops seemed to chatter. That wasn't like me just now. I wouldn't have acted that way before I had a raincoat. But now that I had one, did I have to hide from people? Lost in these thoughts, my legs felt heavy, and I found myself fumbling with the large plastic buttons on my raincoat. Glancing back at Uncle Zhang, who was walking towards the train station with raindrops steadily soaking his back, I thought to myself: it was Uncle Zhang's fault for forgetting his raincoat or umbrella on such a rainy day. As for me, this wasn't my only chance to offer help. With that thought, I turned around and walked away.

But Uncle Zhang's back simply wouldn't leave my mind. At that instant, the raindrops on my raincoat appeared to morph into glistening eyes, observing me to gauge my decision on the issue. Eventually, I resolved to act. "Uncle Zhang!" I exclaimed as I hurried towards him and I removed my raincoat.

Upon reaching him, I handed the raincoat to Uncle Zhang, lost for words.

"Don't bother, don't bother", Uncle Zhang tried to refuse my offering of the raincoat. "I was escorting my granddaughter to Beijing for her music college entrance exam, and we were sharing an umbrella. Then we bumped into your teacher, Ms. Du, and she was with a pile of homework. We gave her our umbrella. I thought of returning home for another one, but I worried we'd be late, so we gave it up."

I was at a loss for words, so I handed over the raincoat and darted off. After a bit of running, it dawned on me to call out to Uncle Zhang, "No need to fret, I've still got a large straw hat!"

I went home, put on my straw hat, and ran in the rain with my chest puffed out.

"Wang Leilei, Wang Leilei!" A sharp voice

called out to me from behind. I turned my head and saw Zhao Xiaoyun!

She ran up and let out half of her "cloak style" raincoat for me, saying, "Why are you wearing a straw hat? Where's your new raincoat?"

"I... umm... over there," Actually I did not want to tell her, but I was afraid that Zhao Xiaoyun thought I was lying, so I pointed in the direction of the train station.

In the distance, my raincoat had melded into a sea of raincoats in an array of colors: pink, sky blue, light green, and milky yellow. Alongside the red and yellow umbrellas, they resembled clusters of blossoming flowers amidst the rain.

2

A Thousand Pieces of Candy Wrappers

During my first-grade summer vacation, I visited my grandmother's residence in Beijing. I was at that age when the adage "At seven or eight, children are a nuisance" rings true. My laughter and chatter echoed through my grandmother's courtyard. On top of that, a girl named Shixiang from the neighborhood befriended me, and the multitude of games we played added to the liveliness and restlessness of my grandmother's house.

We played elastic band skipping in the courtyard, stomping loudly on the blue bricks; we played "catching pebbles" at the square table beneath a jujube tree, the "sheep knuckles" clattering on the table with a series of rustling sounds; we raised bamboo poles high to knock down jujubes for eating, and the green jujubes tumbled across the ground; we competed in singing, with her voice high, mine had to be higher. A lady in my grandmother's house, whom I addressed as cousin aunt, remarked to us: "Do you know what it means to be tired?" Shixiang and I exchanged glances and burst into laughter without reason—there was no humor in the question, yet we laughed uncontrollably, struggling to catch our breath. Yes, what did it mean to be tired? We never dwell on feeling tired. Sometimes, when we heard adults exclaim, "Oh, I'm so tired," we assumed it was because they were adults, and "feeling tired" seemed so distant from us.

When our laughter subsided, my aunt again remarked, "Doesn't Shixiang have a collection of candy wrappers? Why don't you collect more?" I recalled that Shixiang had indeed shared her collection of candy wrappers with me. They were a few dozen, featuring exquisite glass-like transparent designs, neatly tucked between the pages of a slim book. However, I had never grown much interest in her collection, nor did I intend to value my aunt's suggestion. The aunt, too, was a guest at Grandma's, staying there to recover from her illness.

However, Shixiang was intrigued and

queried my aunt, "Why do you suggest us to collect the candy wrappers?" Aunt explained that once we gathered a certain number of candy wrappers, we could exchange them for something special. For instance, a thousand pieces of wrappers could be swapped for an electric toy dog. Shixiang and I were astounded by my aunt's revelation: we had both spotted this new toy at the department store. The little fluffy dog would trot towards you, yapping, once you activated it with batteries inside. Nowadays, an electric dog might not be considered a novelty treasure for children. Yet, over twenty years ago, in a time when the kinds of toys in China were very limited and monotonous, my aunt's promise was enough to thrill us for quite a while. What a treasure that would be! How much delight it would bring! And not to mention this wealth and happiness would be earned through our own efforts.

I eagerly inquired of my aunt who I should approach exchange candy wrappers for an electric dog, while Shixiang sought clarification on the required colour and design of the wrappers. Aunt specified that the wrappers needed to be transparent, each one flat and smooth without any creases. She explained that once we gathered enough wrappers that met these criteria and handed them over, she would assist us in exchanging them for the electric dog.

A thousand pieces of candy wrappers equated to an electric dog. If both Shixiang and I desired one, it meant we needed two thousand wrappers. It was no small amount, but we both were filled with confidence.

From that moment onward, Shixiang and I

refrained from playing games like jumping the rubber band, munching on jujubes, catching "Catching Pebbles," nor singing in competitive singing matches. Grandma's courtyard was restored to its peaceful state, and we began our search journey for candy wrappers earnestly.

When today's children have grown weary of various milk candies and fruit candies, we, during that era, were brimming with endless fascination for candies. Candy wasn't something you always found in your coat pocket, and candy wrappers—especially those delicate transparent glass wrappers from upscale milk candies—were not commonplace at all. Initially, Shixiang and I spent all our pocket money on buying candies, yet we could only afford a few. Despite the discomfort in our throats caused by bingeing on these candies for their wrappers, we scoured the streets, hunting for discarded wrappers in corners and crevices. Sometimes, we would chase after a candy wrapper twirling in the breeze, spending half a day navigating through alleys; we would linger by the candy counter in grocery stores, patiently awaiting adults who brought their children to purchase candies. The moment they bought candies and unwrapped one to place in their child's mouth, we swiftly retrieved the fallen wrapper from the ground, be it from "Shanghai Toffee" or "Cream Coffee". We even attended a wedding celebration of one of Shixiang's relatives, where candy wrappers were strewn across the floor. This brought us immense joy. We wished fervently that all adults would tie the knot during those days, and that all wedding ceremonies would extend invitations to us!

We took those crumpled candy wrappers home, soaked them in a basin to flatten them, and then stuck them on the glass window to dry. After they dried, we carefully peeled them off, and the wrappers were as flat and new as ever.

The summer vacation was about to end. Shixiang and I finally had each collected a thousand candy wrappers. One afternoon, when my aunt was waking up after her nap and drinking a cup of tea, we presented her with two thousand candy wrappers.

My aunt appeared puzzled and asked about what was going on. We exclaimed, "We're collecting wrappers for the electric dog!" She paused briefly, then erupted into laughter, unable to contain herself, gasping for breath. After finally regaining composure, wiping away her tears, she confessed, "It was a jest. I simply grew weary of your incessant clamor in the courtyard."

Shixiang glanced at me, her eyes brimming with sorrow and desolation. I sensed a hint of reproach in her gaze, perhaps directed at me because it was my aunt who had mocked us. At that instant, I was struck by a profound weariness, experiencing for the first time what adults often referred to as fatigue—a weighty burden on the heart.

Shixiang and I retrieved our candy wrappers and returned to the courtyard. As we reached the gate, I tossed the meticulously collected thousand candy wrappers into the air, sending them fluttering like colorful butterflies carried away by the wind.

As I matured, having delved into numerous books and absorbed a wealth of vocabulary, whenever the word "deception" crossed my path, my mind instinctively connected it with the word "aunt." These two words became so intertwined in my subconsciousness that even the passage of time could not fully disentangle them. This led me to think that adults had the capacity to inflict profound and lasting harm upon children, leaving scars hidden deep within a child's memory.

A child can be criticised, a child can be blamed, but a child cannot be deceived; deception is the most profound form of hurt.

We have grown up into grown-ups, but aren't all grown-ups once children?

3

Kite Fairy

My family resides on the outskirts of the city. Apart from the inconvenience of shopping, nearly everything else is convenient.

In front of our building, there are no other houses, just a vast expanse of vegetable field. Standing by the window, facing the expansive land and vast sky, accompanied by the scents of manure, water, and earth, I come to the realisation that the food I consume daily is indeed genuine, and the water I drink is truly fresh.

There's no need to fret about developers purchasing the vegetable field outside our window to erect new buildings and obstruct our view of the distant sky. Rumour has it that the municipal construction department has devised plans to transform this vegetable field into a park. While this news fills us with a sense of fortune, there's also a tinge of disappointment. A park may not be a groundbreaking addition to the city, but a vegetable field is a rarity. Parks are crafted to entertain and possess an intrinsic allure that draws in citizens deliberately; conversely, vegetable fields do not seek to attract anyone. The vegetables grow quietly and methodically in the earth, imparting fresh vitality to the nearby residents.

In our neighbourhood, residents typically stroll along the dirt paths bordering the fields during the early morning and evening hours. They tread carefully along the ridges between the vegetable plots, understanding the farmers' fondness for their crops and cherishing their sentiments. However, only during the first month of the lunar year, when fertilizer has just been stacked at the field's edge and the vegetable fields still lie vacant, people take to running and frolicking in the open ground with the overhead wind turning warm—this is where kite-flying takes flight.

Not only do nearby residents like us frequent the area, but also young people, children, and the elderly ride their bicycles from downtown to fly kites here. When do they discover and take note of our vegetable field? Although the field does not technically belong to us, my neighbors and I feel a sense of pride in our early claim and adopt a welcoming attitude towards these outside visitors, treating them like distant relatives. This sentiment arises from the first month of the lunar year, with its inherent generosity and the clarity of the land and sky.

My kite was rather ordinary compared to the others, and it was inexpensive, costing only two yuan and fifty cents. It portrayed a rustic fairy with a flat nose and puffy mouth, dressed in a pink gown with yellow ribbons. On her chest were the words, "Kite from Gao Yuxiu in Shakou Village, Handan, Hebei, wholesale discount," along with the postal code and other details. Hence, the maker of this fairy kite was indeed the farmer named Gao Yuxiu from Handan. Despite Gao Yuxiu's simple and crude depiction of the fairy, using extremely monotonous colors, I found myself drawn to it. What led me to choose this kite was precisely the words on the fairy's chest. Its commercial appearance couldn't hide Gao Yuxiu's inherent earthiness. His direct and colloquial wording made me decide that I wanted this fairy.

Before evening, it's the ideal time for kite-flying. The sun shines brightly but not harshly, and the breeze is mild yet robust, devoid of any stormy intensity. I hoisted my fairy kite and jogged on the more and more yielding ground, propelling it upwards into the sky. Nearby neighbors, also engaged in kite-flying, cheered me on, saying, "Let out more string! Quickly, let out more string! What a lovely breeze..."

"Let out the string! Let out the string! Let out the string!" What a delightful breeze!

These chants, akin to a labour anthem, resounded in my ears, echoing through the early spring air. The silk string smoothly slipped from the reel in my hand as I watched back and looked up at the ascending fairy. I must admit, this fairy was brimming with vitality: how swiftly she rose with the wind! The air currents at higher altitudes were steadier than those below, allowing her to maintain stability once caught in the wind above.

I focused intently on the fairy kite dancing in the sky, deftly and cautiously releasing the string from my grasp. In that moment, I couldn't help but feel that nothing in the world resembled a fairy more than this kite fairy: her humble appearance was suddenly transformed into an unattainable mystery against the vast expanse of blue sky; her simple attire took on a magnificent and ethereal quality in the wind; and her posture exuded a serene charm. As I looked around, the sky was teeming with black swallows, brown eagles, colorful butterflies, and silver dragons... Why did these paper creatures seem more alive than their real counterparts once they took flight from human hands? It was as if the wind in the heavens granted them a free soul beyond human understanding, and it appeared that only in the sky could they find their own vibrant essence. It was their living essence that bestowed joy and good fortune upon us on the ground.

"Let out the string! Let out the string! Let out the string!" What a lovely breeze!

Occasionally, amidst our group of kite flyers, some peculiar individuals would appear: an Audi would screech to a stop at the field's edge, and two or three stylishly dressed men and women would step out of the car, encircling a young man adorned with a diamond ring. The young man, the kite's owner, was pleased to keep his hands free—others held the kite for him. It was a colossal and luxurious centipede-shaped kite, custom-made from Weifang, Shandong. Its reel wasn't a simple poplar stick like the one I held, but a sophisticated contraption with a pulley and a silk line shimmering with dignified silver light. The "Diamond Ring" individual stood aloof, gazing disdainfully at the sky, while my fairy and my neighbor's swallow soared above. He extracted a cigarette from his pocket, and immediately someone lit it for him. A lady, struggling in high heels, hurried over to "Diamond Ring" and offered him a tin of "Coconut Wind." The grandiose display truly left us in awe.

Then, the centipede began its slow ascent into the wind, its beauty exceptional. Cheers erupted all around, and some kind souls forgave the "Diamond Ring" for his arrogance with sincere applause. However, I felt a twinge of pity for him. He never laid a hand on the centipede or the kite string. Only when his attendant had launched the centipede into the blue sky did he drop his cigarette and take the reel from the attendant's hand. His demeanor was far from that of a skilled helmsman; rather, his stance in the field resembled that of a spoiled child. Such a child would be too lazy to crack sunflower seeds by himself, finding happiness only when adults cracked each seed and placed it right into his mouth.

Then, a memory surfaced of a driver from my workplace who had a passion for kite-flying. One day, during the first month of the lunar year, as we were on a car trip, he shared with me a childhood tale. Growing up in the countryside, he had the skill to craft kites but lacked the means to buy proper string. Instead, he used the thread from quilts dismantled by his mother to replace the kite string. Connecting the threads together resulted in numerous weak joints, rendering it unstable. On one occasion, while his kite soared in the sky, the makeshift string snapped, sending the kite adrift with the wind. He embarked on a pursuit, racing along the country road for seven or eight miles to retrieve his lost kite.

Who nowadays would run seven or eight miles to chase a kite? It's worth just a few yuan. Perhaps a young man with a luxurious centipede kite might consider chasing it, sending someone in his Audi to pursue it.

But if someone were truly chasing a kite in an Audi, it would feel more like threatening the centipede in the sky with a vehicle on the ground.

I realized my attention had wavered, and then my kite string snapped. The wind lifted the fairy kite briefly before dropping it, causing it to sway as it drifted into the distance. As dusk descended, I set out to pursue my fairy kite, traversing fertilized fields, countless furrows and ridges, the crisscrossing ruts of the dirt road, and the apathetic gazes of "Diamond rings". My determination never wavered, as this chase was solely between the fairy and me, unrelated to others. As nightfall approached and sounds faded, I finally clambered onto the roof of a pigsty and discovered the fairy kite lying there, slightly tilted. I felt a deep connection to this kite as if it were a long-lost friend, perhaps bearing the surname Gao, part of the same lineage as Farmer Gao Yuxiu from Shakou Village in Handan.

Suddenly, a large and round moon hung heavily in the sky, casting its glow upon me as I contemplated the true essence of flying a kite. Yet, I found myself without an answer.

However, through the broken kite string, the vanishing fairy, my pursuit, and eventual recovery, I came to realise that joy is something I attain with my own efforts, through sincere and earnest pursuit of my heart's desires. The connection of the peaceful mind between humans on the ground and the fairy in the heaven actually isn't the kite string sold in the market.

4

Communicating with Strangers

Years ago, I resided close to my middle school, just a ten-minute walk away. Each morning, as part of my routine, I'd pause at a snack shop along the way to buy breakfast.

I was thirteen years old and in my first year of junior high school. It was a time when we were encouraged to "dig tunnels deep, stockpile grain extensively." Consequently, at the start of this semester, we began learning about soil excavation, brickmaking, and air raid shelter construction. Although subjects like Chinese and mathematics were on the curriculum, they didn't carry as much weight as activities like digging soil, with open-book exams fostering an atmosphere where studying seemed optional. Only the newly introduced subject of "Agriculture" demonstrated its significance. During each lesson, the teacher stressed that this subject was crucial for our future. Thus, despite my ignorance of Ampere or Volt, I learned about nitrogen, phosphorus, potassium, humanure, firewood ash fertilizer, flowering periods, pollination, yam beds, etc. However, the knowledge about agriculture from books failed to truly ignite my passion, or perhaps I was reluctant to become a genuine farmer. My body was ready to endure strenuous physical labor at a young age, while my mind remained vacant. If I wasn't destined to be a farmer in the future, then what would I become? I had no answer to that question.

Every morning, I strolled to school with a blank mind, pausing at the snack shop where I indulged in youtiao (also known as "fried dough sticks") and soy milk. The shop bustled with activity, a 5-inch iron pot positioned outside bubbling with oil as it crisped the dough, the air carrying a delicate hint of cottonseed fragrance. This oil, derived from refined cottonseed oil, despite undergoing purification to remove impurities, still emitted wisps of smoke during frying. In a city where each person had a monthly quota of merely 150 grams of cooking oil, savoring youtiao fried in defatted cottonseed oil was like a celebration. I queued patiently, observing the skilled and swift movements of the cook.

The young girl responsible for frying the dough stood by the pot, wielding a pair of long bamboo chopsticks. With skillful precision, she flipped the dough sticks at just the right moment, transferring the perfectly fried ones into a wire basket nearby to drain the excess oil—a crucial step due to the preciousness of oil. She didn't need to make eye contact with the customers, solely focused on her task with lowered eyelids, seamlessly flipping and transferring. Her movements exuded joy, and her agility was evident in this pleasant labor. Occasionally, as she raised her face to wipe away sweat, I noticed her striking beauty. Her fresh complexion, chestnut hair peeking out from her white cap, and her pure, focused gaze—everything about her left me at a loss for words. The allure of a mature woman stirred conflicting emotions within me, blending self-doubt with hope.

Back then, my understanding of beauty was quite limited. Even the few images I had encountered felt distant and otherworldly. I recall a neighbor's child owning a forgotten copy of the comic book "Amelia," a treasure from before the Cultural Revolution. While the tragic narrative of beauty by Shakespeare intrigued me, I didn't perceive Amelia as beautiful. Additionally, we had a few old records at home, featuring exquisite album covers that once left me mesmerized: the elegant dance of Odette from "Swan Lake" and Mr. Yuan Yunfu's decorative and charming portrait of girls on "Solveig's Song"... They all embodied beauty, yet remained unattainable. It was only the girl who fried dough sticks, a lively and tangible beauty I could sense and grasp, who filled my previously empty notions of beauty. She made me realize my own womanhood and inspired me to grow into a beauty like her.

In the ensuing mornings, I queued up and began to observe her keenly: the way she plaited her hair, her posture while standing, her gesture to wipe away sweat, the sandals adorning her feet, and the white cloth cap atop her head. As I emulated her by tightly plaiting my own ponytail, I felt the gap between us narrow. During the chilly winter days, when I wore a scarf and intentionally let a few strands of hair escape, joy instantly filled my heart. My days became more engaging as I mimicked her, and my mind was no longer vacant. As I gazed at the "nitrogen," "phosphorus," and "potassium" on the blackboard, I sensed a newfound identity blossoming within me.

Later, we moved to a new place, and eventually, I really went to that vast land with the coal and wood fertilizers and the yam beds. I could no longer visit that snack shop.

As I encountered new brides along rural roads or in farmers' courtyards, I subconsciously compared them to the girl who fried dough sticks, firmly believing none could match her. Several years later, upon returning to the city, I happened upon that same snack shop and found the girl still there. The 5-inch iron pot still bubbled, and she continued to stir with long bamboo chopsticks. Her chestnut hair had been cut short, fluttering around the oil-stained edge of her white hat. She still wiped her sweat with a familiar gesture. Yet, when she looked up, it was hard to discern whether her face was naturally rosy or flushed from the stove's heat. She had lost

044

her previous joy, and her once-agile figure now lacked its former grace. Indifferently glancing at the customers in line, she chewed something carelessly, her actions lacking focus and professionalism, as if she had chewed the dough sticks herself. From an adult perspective, I stood before the pot observing the elder her. For the first time, I questioned the aesthetic standards of my youth, because the woman before me was just ordinary. She pulled the chopsticks from the pot, pointing at me and saying, "Hey, go to the back of the line to buy the dough sticks!" Her voice was slightly hoarse, her eyes tired and irritable. It seemed she hadn't known happiness for many years, suffering from the torment of smoke and the frying pan.

I hurried towards the "back" she had indicated, as if leaving behind an untold story, one I had never shared with anyone, and as if fearing to be exposed: that's the type of woman I admired back then.

Many years later, I'd encountered numerous beautiful women, both Chinese and foreign, old and young... The dough stick cook couldn't hold a candle to them. Occasionally, I reflected on this, almost as if to reaffirm how naive I was as a teenager.

Again, many years later, no longer naive, I revisited the snack shop. It was an autumn afternoon when the van I was travelling in broke down in front of the shop. Only a quiet oil pot sat at the entrance, so I walked inside. I found her sitting alone behind the counter, still wearing the now-greyed white hat, stained by smoke. Her gaze was vacant, and she occasionally yawned, showing signs of exhaustion. There was no enthusiasm on her face, no restlessness nor irritability; it seemed as though she had devoted her entire life to the shop and the counter. On the counter, there were some wilting pickles. I estimated that she was about forty years old at most.

The afternoon sunlight flooded the shop with a golden hue, casting the hard plastic table cover in a warm and soft glow. I felt an overwhelming urge to confide to the woman, who was yawning behind the counter, about my admiration for her from many years ago.

"When I was a child, I used to buy youtiao here," I said.

"There are none now," she replied indifferently.

"You used to stand in front of the pot every day," I said.

"What do you want to buy? We only have bean buns now," she interrupted me.

"You had two thick and long plaits, wearing white sandals, and you..."

"What do you really want?" She almost blamed me for interrupting her daze, turning her face away from me.

"I just wanted to tell you that I used to think you were the most beautiful person, and I tried to dress up like you."

"Huh?" She turned her face back to me in surprise.

The van's horn was blaring, signaling that the car was fixed, and the driver was urging me to get in it.

I hurried out of the snack shop, grappling for a reason behind my sudden confession and feeling let down by the disjointed conversation we had. However, I couldn't shake off the memory of her "Huh" and the expression on her face when she finally glanced at me. I wished to believe that she took the compliment from a stranger to heart.

Soon, on another lively and bustling morning, I drove past the snack shop once more. The oil pot at the entrance was bubbling, and she was still deftly handling the dough sticks with bamboo chopsticks. A fresh, white hat adorned her head, and her chestnut curls cascaded down from beneath the hat's brim. The newly permed hair lent a lively and charming air to her face. Tough in her plump figure, she was striving to capture the agility of her youth, which carried a more mature grace.

As the car swiftly passed the shop, I suddenly realized the reason behind my impulsive confession that afternoon. It was because I was no longer naive that I dared to express gratitude to a woman who had sparked my youthful appreciation for beauty.

In doing so, I hoped to rekindle her own love for beauty.

There probably wouldn't be a banner at the entrance of the snack shop saying "Welcome the Health Inspection Team." The city's food industry routinely welcomes inspection teams periodically. Could there be a camera positioned at the front of the snack shop? Perhaps a television drama crew had chosen the shop as a filming location. I felt fortunate that my car had just passed by, and I held firm in my belief that her rejuvenation stemmed from her understanding of my gratitude.

When you set aside your vanity and approach strangers, every aspect of your ordinary life becomes infused with the charm of unfamiliar faces.

5

The Faint Afterglow

In the spring of 2001, I welcomed the Miyoshi Ikezawa family to my home in Hebei. Mr. Ikezawa, a Japanese professor at Fukushima University, was not yet fifty and had dedicated many years to studying contemporary Chinese literature and translating my novels. His wife, Mashiro, was a friendly computer teacher at a middle school who enjoyed playing the piano. Their son, Takeru, was in junior high school. My friendship with Ikezawa had spanned a decade since he was hired as a Japanese teacher at a local university in Hebei and settled in my city. Upon our initial meeting, Mr. and Mrs. Ikezawa graciously invited me to their home, where Mrs. Ikezawa performed a tea ceremony. Her intricate hairstyle, the fragrant tea, and the green grass in the antique porcelain vase created a serene and pure atmosphere that left a lasting impression on me, inspiring my essay "Grass Ring." I reciprocated by inviting the Ikezawa family to my house, where our gatherings were always joyous, especially for four-year-old Takeru, who seemed to find comfort in my family's company—perhaps due to his loneliness at school. Mr. Ikezawa shared that Takeru's only friend was the son of the school's cafeteria cook, and Takeru often joined him in climbing the coal pile near the kitchen door. Adjusting to the local environment was challenging for Takeru, who suffered from mosquito bites that left several small red bumps on his face and arms. Our gatherings were further enhanced by my father's exceptional cooking and my parents' warm hospitality towards our guests, leading to these delightful meetings continuing until the Ikezawa family's departure from China a year later. During their stay, Mr. Ikezawa also introduced two of his Japanese colleagues to my home, one of whom was particularly fond of drinking. During a meal, he spotted a bottle of Japanese sake called "Kikumasamune" in our liquor cabinet and eagerly requested a taste. I obliged, offering him the "Kikumasamune" gifted to me by another Japanese friend. As he indulged, he occasionally sighed in intoxication and then, reminiscent of his homeland, began to sing with tears in his eyes—a heartfelt rendition of folk tunes steeped in homesickness.

After the guests had departed that evening, my father recounted a memory triggered by Mr. Ikezawa and his friends' song at the dinner table. Fifty years ago, he was a village boy on the Central Hebei Plain, where a small squad of Japanese soldiers, about twenty to thirty in number, was stationed near their village. Each evening, these soldiers would march in formation, singing the same song without fail. Clad in combat helmets, carrying Type 38 Rifles, they raised their right hands high as they marched in unison, their boots thudding on the yellow earth beneath. Dust swirled around them, and their singing resembled a thunderous roar. It was the identical march and song every single day. Over time, my father learned the lyrics and melody, yet he never grasped its significance. He believed their song must be linked to the War of Resistance against Japanese Aggression. Their singing wasn't for amusement; rather, it was akin to the steel helmets they wore, the bayonets on their shoulders, and the boots they marched in—tools of their subjugation of the Chinese populace. What else could the daily song of a military unit be but a rallying cry to spur these soldiers to invade other countries? This melody became a haunting presence in his heart, a perpetual source of unease. He confided that he had wanted to interrupt the singing at the dinner table to inquire of the Japanese guests whether they were aware that the old song was routinely sung by a Japanese military unit stationed in a Hebei village during the harsh year of 1942. For fifty years, my father harbored a curiosity about the song's true meaning.

I said to my father, "Why don't you ask Mr. Ikezawa?" My father replied, "It would inevitably make Mr. Ikezawa embarrassed." Our conversation stopped.

But from that day on, the song seemed to be rekindled in my father's mind, and sometimes he could even hum a few lines. It was around the time when the Ikezawa family returned to their home country, my father expressed his regret, saying, "Why do we always consider others? It would have been better to ask at that time."

Ten years have passed.

This time, when Mr. Ikezawa and his family returned to China, visiting my home was a significant part of their trip.

Additionally, Mr. Ikezawa wished to discuss some details regarding the publication of my second collection of short stories, which he had translated into Japanese. Over the past decade, the one who had undergone the most change was their son, Takeru. Now, Takeru, a bright and courteous young man, was nearly as tall as his father. Witnessing a child's growth compelled me to acknowledge the passing of time. Unfortunately, Takeru had no recollection of his time in China and couldn't remember the son of the cafeteria cook from his childhood. It was only through his parents' recounting that he learned he had once lived in China as a child.

After being apart for a considerable time, we all indulged in nostalgia about the past. While I knew the Ikezawa family appreciated Chinese cuisine, given the numerous Japanese restaurants in our city, I arranged for us to sample Chinese-style Japanese cuisine. Contemporary Chinese-style Japanese restaurants not only offer a variety of Japanese sake brands but also feature plum wine, a favourite among Japanese women. As we raised our glasses in a toast, we fondly recalled the half bottle of "Kikumasamune" we had shared a decade ago at my home. During the meal, Mr. and Mrs. Ikezawa continually expressed their amazement at the transformation in China. However, it was at that moment that I noticed my father acting oddly; he grew less talkative and his responses to the Ikezawas' remarks were distracted and perfunctory, a departure from his usual warmth. It was then that my father whispered to me, "I'm ready to ask about that song now." Since my father was determined, I felt this was an opportune moment. After all, a restaurant provides a neutral setting, akin to a neutral country amid a war between nations, offering less of a familiar ambiance and fewer chances for discomfort.

My father began by mentioning Takeru's age without apparent reason. He recounted that during the War of Resistance against Japanese Aggression, he himself was even younger than Takeru, yet the war had a profound impact on his life. He shared an incident when Japanese soldiers raided the village, capturing him as a hostage and nearly throwing him into a burning tunnel.

I observed that Mr. and Mrs. Ikezawa had set aside their chopsticks and were sitting upright, their gaze lowered, displaying a touch of guilt and nervousness. My father, attuned to the mood, remarked, "What I wish to inquire of Mr. Ikezawa does not pertain to the war, but rather a song that has intrigued me for numerous years." With that, my father hummed the tune of the song and recounted the scene of the Japanese soldiers singing in the past: their raised arms, the ochre earth yielding beneath their boots... the thunderous roars and determined march.

Following that, Mr. and Mrs. Ikezawa's demeanors gradually shifted. They both experienced a sense of relief. Mrs. Ikezawa was the swiftest to react, eagerly informing my father that it was a well-known nursery rhyme in Japan, adorned with a truly beautiful melody, often sung by children of their era as they journeyed homeward from school. "But they sang it with the wrong cadence," she remarked, alluding to the Japanese soldiers who marched with their firearms. "It ought to be like this," Mrs. Ikezawa elucidated, making gestures with her hands as she sang the song anew. Upon her conclusion, Mr. Ikezawa translated the lyrics for my father. The song was dubbed *The Faint Afterglow*, and the lyrics, roughly interpreted, narrated the emergence of the afterglow, the darkening of the sky, the temple bells resonating from the mountain, and everyone returning home hand in hand, reminiscent of crows winging their way back to their nests...

As it turned out, the Japanese soldiers were singing a Japanese nursery rhyme, a revelation that caught my father off guard. What surprised him even more was how the soldiers had transformed the lyrical 4/4 rhythm of the nursery rhyme into a march tempo, imbuing it with raw hostility. My father's recounting of this and the trauma it evoked in his mind left Mr. and Mrs. Ikezawa feeling uneasy. In an effort to alter my father's perception of the nursery rhyme, they joined together in singing the correct version of *The Faint Afterglow*, a truly beautiful and melodious song.

After supper, the Ikezawa family joined us at my abode for tea. To alleviate the slightly strained and uneasy atmosphere lingering from the dinner table, we refrained from mentioning *The Faint Afterglow*. Instead, our conversation veered towards literature, the evolving landscape of China, until the hour grew late and Takeru began to nod off. With the guests preparing to take their leave, as they donned their shoes and hats in the hallway, Mrs. Ikezawa abruptly departed from her husband and son, hurrying to the piano in the living room. With a hint of excitement, she beckoned my father, "Mr.

Tie Yang, let's render the song once more before our departure!" Then, she settled at the piano and accompanied my father. Together, they sang *The Faint Afterglow* in its original rhythm, capturing its innate poetic and serene essence. Observing Mrs. Ikezawa's graceful figure on the piano bench, I comprehended her intentions. She was resolute in restoring the song's honor, dispelling the shadow it had once cast upon my father's heart.

It was a poignant moment, and if one were to metaphorically depict the tranquil essence of humanity, it would be encapsulated in two individuals from different nations harmonizing in song, bridging hearts through a nursery rhyme.

Shortly thereafter, when I received an invitation to visit Japan from the Japan-China Cultural Exchange Association, Mr. Ikezawa made a special journey from Fukushima to Tokyo to meet me. He presented me with a gift for my father—a CD of *The Faint Afterglow*. Thoughtfully, Mr. Ikezawa included the Chinese lyrics and some background information about the song for my father.

The Faint Afterglow was composed in 1923 and initially featured in the Japanese publication "Cultural Music Score – New Children's Songs". Swiftly, it garnered widespread acclaim and has remained a staple in the curriculum for first and second-grade students since 1950. The lyrics comprise two verses:

Faint afterglow, faint afterglow,
The day is ending, night is near,
From the temple on the hill, the bells ring clear,

Let's hold hands and head home, dear.

The children are home, the night is calm,
The moon is shining, soft and bright,
As the birds in their dreams take flight,
The stars in the sky start to light up the
night.

The Faint Afterglow has also been rewritten, and the revised lyrics are included in Mr. Tohru Kasagi's laser book series titled Yesterday a Piglet Was Born. The lyric goes like this:

Faint afterglow, faint afterglow,
The sky doesn't darken, no,
The temple bells on the mountain don't ring,
How can the war ever end?
Crows have no homes to return to.

The editor speculates that the lyrics were rewritten around 1942 to 1943. "During that period in Japan," the editor reflects, "despite Hideki Tojo's radio announcements boasting of the Imperial Army's victories, Tokyo and other cities such as Kawasaki, Nagoya, Yokosuka, and Kobe were being bombed by the Americans. This led Japan swiftly into a wartime state. Severe shortages prompted the government to enact the 'Regulations for the Production and Sale of Luxury Goods,' advocating that 'Luxury is the enemy.' Items such as precious metals, jewelry, clothing, silverware, and cameras were deemed luxuries. Even long sleeves were seen as extravagant, sparking a movement to 'shorten sleeves.' Simultaneously, neon lights and women's hair perming were banned, and gender-bending performers in dance halls vanished." The editor also recalls the widespread collection of iron kettles, swords, copper products, and even temple bells from elementary school grounds during that period. "Meat, vegetables, and rice became incredibly scarce," the editor adds, "plunging society into a barren existence: devoid of temple bells, devoid of the sunset's glow, with crows left homeless, amidst the enduring specter of war."

So, the rewritten lyrics are no longer just a simple nursery rhyme. They become a cry against war and a call for peace.

Upon our return home, my father and I listened to the CD of *The Faint Afterglow* numerous times. Sung by the renowned Japanese vocalists Yasuda Sachiko and Saori Yuki in a duet, they conveyed pure and exquisite emotion with their simple, unembellished tones. It struck me that a simple longing for home could be heart-wrenching. But what of the Japanese soldiers who sang this song during the invasion of China six decades ago? In the evening, they fervently repeated "The Faint Afterglow," their voices filled with longing to return home. Yet in the daytime, they could mercilessly coerce a Chinese boy into a fiery tunnel. Perhaps it's not entirely surprising, considering there were Japanese army recruits, some studying liberal arts, who carried Lu Xun's novels in their pockets during the invasion of China.

I observed that fourteen-year-old Takeru refrained from joining the adults in singing *The Faint Afterglow* that night. I pondered whether this age-old song still found its place in the music textbooks of Japanese elementary schools in the new century. Perhaps Takeru's reluctance stemmed from the typical shyness of a boy on the brink of adolescence. It's possible that he and his peers simply weren't interested in this old nursery rhyme, nor were they familiar with the history of The War of Resistance against Japanese Aggression from the last century. In my experience in Japan, I've noticed that many young people don't have a taste for sushi or miso soup; they exhibit more enthusiasm for McDonald's and French cuisine. However, I firmly believe that *The Faint Afterglow* holds its own value, encapsulating the most fundamental and universal longing of humanity: the desire to return to one's own home.

6

Gold and Diamonds

Lincoln-Douglas Elementary School is a public school located in Freeport, Illinois. One hundred and thirty-five years ago, the Republican Abraham Lincoln and his Democratic rival, Stephen Douglas, engaged in several spirited debates here. Lincoln was renowned for his shrewdness, quick wit, and sense of justice, making him one of the most distinguished lawyers in Illinois. On the other hand, Douglas, despite his stature, was known as the "little giant." He was a celebrated and eloquent orator, dedicating his life to advocating American Expansionism. The outcome of the election saw Lincoln emerge victorious over all his opponents, securing his position as the sixteenth President of the United States. His famous speech, The Emancipation Proclamation, further solidified his legacy as one of the greatest presidents in American history. One can only imagine the magnitude of interest the debates between these two remarkable figures generated among voters in Illinois at that time. Even today, two bronze statues stand in front of an American fast-food restaurant in Freeport, depicting their intense debates. This location holds significance as the small square in front of the fast-food restaurant was the actual site of their historic discussions. The decision to name the city's elementary school Lincoln-Douglas serves as a fitting tribute to these two illustrious Illinoisans and their impactful legacy.

This afternoon, I received an invitation to visit the elementary school. The principal who welcomed me was a kind, middle-aged blonde woman. She informed me that the students had never encountered a Chinese individual before, and my presence had sparked great excitement among them. She mentioned that they would likely have numerous questions for me. Regrettably, I explained to the principal that I could only spare sixty minutes as I had another commitment following my visit to the school. Undeterred, the principal assured me, "I've made arrangements for you. To accommodate the various grades within the limited time, we've selected one class from each grade, from fourth to first, and you'll have fifteen minutes to engage with each class. What do you think?" Finding the principal's plan quite reasonable, I happily agreed and commenced my "circuit" between the different classes, accompanied by the principal.

Upon entering the fourth-grade classroom, my attention was immediately drawn to the colorful ribbons adorning the walls, adorned with the unfamiliar yet endearing Chinese characters for "China" and "lady". It was a simple yet heartfelt gesture of welcome from a small-town school with limited knowledge of China. Approaching the blackboard, where a large world map hung prominently, I began my introduction by stating my name and informing the students that China, situated in Asia, boasted a population of 1.2 billion.

Gesturing to the map, I pointed out Hebei Province as my place of origin, inviting questions from the eager faces before me. Addressing the class, I said, "I've heard that you have many questions for me, and I'm more than happy to answer them now." The teacher, in turn, encouraged the students, remarking, "Mrs. Tie Ning will only be with us for fifteen minutes, so please don't hesitate to ask her questions." With those words, the classroom erupted with enthusiasm, and almost every one of the twenty students eagerly raised their hands, eager to inquire. Their questions predominantly began with "China": "How many holidays does China have?" "Do people in China celebrate Christmas?" "How many types of vehicles are there in China?" "Do cars in China have automatic transmissions?" "How many children are there in a Chinese family?" "Do adults in China allow their children to feed small animals?" "Why do people in China still eat rice at night?" "Is Chinese easy to learn?" "Which language do you use to write novels?" "Can you tell us a story you've written?" One particularly enthusiastic boy even exclaimed, "Does China have Chinese restaurants? We have one here, and the food is delicious!" From this barrage of questions, I could sense the students' eagerness to learn about China and their realization of their limited knowledge about it. I answered their inquiries as succinctly and clearly as possible, offering insights into the lives of adults and children in contemporary China. They listened intently, occasionally expressing wonder and amazement. When they requested a story of my own, I spent five minutes recounting my short novel, titled *Ah, Xiangxue.* The tale of the beautiful and pure-souled Chinese girl, Xiangxue, left the children silent, with a few girls' eyes brimming with tears.

Fifteen minutes flew by swiftly, and upon exiting the classroom, I found myself surrounded by students, showering me with hugs and kisses. Many children handed me small notes, each adorned with the heartfelt message: "I love you!" The teacher expressed to me that this encounter would be cherished as an unforgettable moment. She wanted me to understand that the Chinese characters displayed on the classroom's ribbon were meticulously crafted by her and her students over three days. Even for adults like her, mastering Chinese proved to be a formidable task. Nevertheless, the students in her class were on the verge of embarking on their journey to learn Chinese, and my visit, along with our discussion, had ignited within them a profound eagerness to delve deeper into the realm of China.

Following that, I proceeded to visit the third and second grades. Upon entering the second-grade classroom, I was greeted with a display of Japanese etiquette as all the students rose to their feet, offering their salutations with hands clasped. The enthusiasm of these two classes surpassed even that of the previous one, as they eagerly fired off questions, sometimes not even waiting for my responses, engaging in lively debates amongst themselves about the queries posed. For instance, one boy inquired, "Does China have an ocean?" Another boy promptly interjected, asserting, "Of course, it does," citing his observation of a Chinese family dining on fish on television. To him, the presence of fish implied the existence of an ocean in China.

Finally, I reached the first-grade classroom, which I must admit was exceedingly cosy, resembling more of a small recreation area. The desks and chairs were not meticulously arranged; rather, they were scattered around the room's periphery. Soft carpet adorned the floor, upon which the students sat in a relaxed manner, surrounded by toys strewn about. I exchanged greetings with the students seated on the floor, and one seven-year-old lad clad in black lantern pants rose to his feet, informing me that he was donning traditional Chinese attire and learning Chinese kung fu from a Japanese instructor, hence his desire to greet me in a Chinese manner. With that, he executed a deep bow. His classmates erupted into applause in response. Another student promptly shared that his family also had ties to China, mentioning, "We have a pair of Chinese chopsticks at home, although sadly, I've yet to master their use." A bespectacled boy then asserted rather solemnly, "I possess some knowledge about China. It's my belief that Chinese families should have fewer children because the more offspring they have, the more dwellings they'll require. Just imagine the number of trees that would need to be felled for all those homes! It could upset the ecological balance, leading to disaster." It was quite astonishing to hear such insights from a seven-year-old American regarding China's population and ecological concerns. I commended the boy, remarking, "Your analysis is astute, and the issue you've raised is one that our government is actively addressing." Another slender lad, unwilling to be overshadowed, chimed in, "I reckon China and India are both remarkable nations due to their extensive histories." I quipped back, "You're like a miniature historian!" This elicited laughter from the students.

As I responded to the pupils' inquiries and listened to their perspectives, I observed an intriguing occurrence: during my interactions with the younger classes, there appeared to be a noticeable uptick in the children's knowledge regarding China. This piqued my curiosity, prompting me to contemplate delving deeper into the matter with them. Regrettably, my visit had exceeded the allocated sixty minutes, necessitating my departure to avoid disrupting my subsequent engagement. As I bid farewell to the students and exited the premises, pupils from all four-year groups assembled to see me off. Among them was a fair-haired, blue-eyed lad, accompanied by his peers, who approached me at the school gate and presented me with a small token. It comprised a miniature bronze-cast, gold-plated toy horse, measuring five centimeters in length, featuring a majestic horn protruding from its head and a "diamond"-adorned belly, reminiscent of a figure from ancient mythology. The boy, his gaze sincere yet tinged with shyness, quickly retreated after offering the gift, seemingly apprehensive of my reaction. Gratefully, I accepted the little horse and proceeded to bestow a kiss upon the child.

On my journey back, I found myself once again gazing at the small war horse nestled in my palm. Beneath the resplendent hues of the setting sun, the horse exuded a gentle warmth. It dawned on me that I had neglected to inquire about the boy's name, yet upon reflection, I realized that what truly lingered in my memory was the innocence reflected in the children's eyes. Basking in the purity of their gaze is indeed a blessing; it possesses the power to cleanse the dust accumulated from our adult lives, often fraught with battles and challenges.

Upon my return home, one of my American acquaintances chanced upon the gold-plated miniature horse adorned with a "diamond". Recounting the tale behind it, I explained its significance. In response, he remarked, "I'm certain that the lad bestowed upon you his most treasured possession." Reflecting on his own boyhood experiences, he shared a personal anecdote: of a time when he unearthed a translucent stone in his backyard, firmly convinced of its immense value, believing it to be worth six million dollars. Consequently, he had clandestinely safeguarded the stone for many years.

It could be asserted that the gift bestowed upon me by the lad from Freeport was indeed his equivalent of gold and diamonds. Perhaps, it stands as the most precious gift I have ever received.

7

A Country Party in Stevenson County

The Hales family resides in Stevenson County, Illinois, where they oversee a modestly sized ranch dedicated to raising cattle and horses. Having journeyed from Chicago, I was graciously invited to spend a brief sojourn with the Hales.

Mr. and Mrs. Hales, both in their seventies, enjoy robust health. During the day, Mr. Hales escorted me to the ranch to acquaint me with their cattle. The pasture stretched out in verdant splendor, with the cows idly roaming about. Among them, two newborn calves, barely a day old, were diligently watched over by their mother. As I endeavored to approach and greet the young ones, the cows swiftly intervened, positioning themselves protectively in front of their offspring while emitting disapproving bellows in my direction. Chuckling, I remarked to Mr. Hales, "Seems mothers all over the world share the same instincts."

On the ranch, Mr. Hales shared his history with me: During World War II, he served in the U.S. Army, preparing for an assault on Japan. However, following the dropping of atomic bombs on Hiroshima and Nagasaki by the United States, Mr. Hales' deployment to

Japan became unnecessary. Subsequently, he pursued higher education, obtaining a master's degree in horticulture. Upon completing his studies, he returned to his hometown to impart his knowledge as a horticulture educator. Scooping up a handful of the rich black soil from the ranch, he remarked to me, "Once I retire, my son wishes to whisk us away to the city but behold this exquisite black soil. Despite being a humble farmer, tending to horses and cattle may not yield great wealth, yet my affection for the land remains unwavering."

Over dinner, Mr. and Mrs. Hales engaged me in a discussion regarding the challenges facing American agriculture. Mr. Hales highlighted that a mere three percent of the U.S. populace is involved in agricultural pursuits, yet a single American farmer has the capacity to nourish 160 compatriots and even contribute to grain exports. This statistic, he remarked optimistically, underscores the efficiency of agricultural production, buoyed by favourable government subsidies. However, he lamented the pressing issue of extensive water and soil depletion, exacerbated by the profit-driven focus of certain large-scale farmers who neglect soil conservation practices. Furthermore, Mr. Hales noted the reluctance of many younger individuals to pursue careers in agriculture, a departure from the traditions of their forebears. Yet, amidst this trend, there are encouraging instances of university graduates returning to their rural roots to bolster agricultural vitality. To illustrate, Mr. and Mrs. Hales introduced me to a female educator who teaches agriculture at a local high school. She has taken the initiative to establish a group comprising several ambitious students aspiring to agricultural careers post-graduation. Together, they advocate tirelessly for the significance of agricultural development in rural areas through various initiatives.

Remarkably, all members of this group have affiliated with the Illinois chapter of the American Association for the Future of Agriculture, an organisation with an illustrious 80-year history in the United States. While the association experienced a period of dormancy, it has recently experienced a resurgence in certain states, indicative of a renewed commitment to advancing agricultural interests.

One day, Mr. and Mrs. Hales informed me about an upcoming county gathering for farmers at the high school cafeteria in the evening. The event, centered around the future of agriculture, was being organized by middle school students from the Stevenson County Agriculture Group. They extended an invitation for me to join them, to which I gladly accepted.

The gathering was indeed distinctive, featuring discussions on American agriculture followed by a lavish dinner. The culinary delights, including the main courses and desserts, were contributed by the attendees themselves, with each family preparing one or two dishes to share with the assembly. Mrs. Hales had commenced her culinary preparations in the afternoon, simmering beef, potatoes, and carrots in a clay pot. She insisted that I sample the dish for its flavor, to which I remarked that it would likely steal the show that evening. In response, Mrs. Hales humbly remarked, "While there may be other exceptional dishes from fellow attendees, the beef from the cattle I've raised is unparalleled in the county."

At seven o'clock in the evening, Mr. and Mrs. Hales and I set off for the county's high school. I carried the electric clay pot while Mrs. Hales bore a wicker basket laden with napkins, cutlery, and plates. Upon arrival, we were greeted by several male and female students attired in blue uniforms, stationed at the entrance. Mr. Hales proceeded to introduce me to the leaders of the agricultural group: a president, two vice presidents, and a secretary. Their uniforms, customized with vibrant embroidered "FFA" (Future Farmers of America) insignias on their chests and right arms, underscored their dedication to their vocation, lending a sense of gravity to the occasion. Observing the youthful leaders, aged around sixteen or seventeen, I noted their neatly coiffed hair and efforts to appear mature with the use of hair gel and wax, yet their countenances retained a semblance of innocent youthfulness. The secretary, a girl adorned with freckles named Balgen, extended a warm welcome, presenting each of us with numbered invitations.

By that juncture, nearly twenty families from Stevenson County had gathered. Among them were couples attending as pairs, parents accompanied by their children, and young mothers cradling infants in their arms. The long dining table was adorned with an array of pots and baskets, while some attendees brought flowers to embellish the stage.

The solemn president rapped the table with a rubber hammer, signaling the commencement of the meeting. The first order of business was for the leaders to present their reports on the agricultural development initiatives undertaken over the past year. As an attentive observer, I found Secretary Balgen's contribution particularly noteworthy. She recounted her journey into agriculture, revealing that her passion ignited during high school, leading her to take charge of caring for the eight horses on her family's property. Frequently, she volunteered her spare time to assist veterinarians in treating livestock for local farmers, even mastering the art of delivering foals through this hands-on experience. Next, a young professor from a state university within the county was invited to expound upon the significance of agricultural development. His eloquence, coupled with poetic descriptions of the symbiotic relationship between the land and its inhabitants, captivated the audience. His blend of humor and profound knowledge of agricultural technology garnered continuous applause, underscoring the relevance of his insights to the community. The subsequent segment involved acknowledging the families and individuals who had lent their support to the agricultural group throughout the year. Each name mentioned by the president elicited a standing ovation and warm greetings from the attendees, including Mr. and Mrs. Hales. A parent representative, none other than the president's mother, delivered an impassioned speech expressing pride in her son and the collective efforts of the agricultural group toward county-wide agricultural advancement. She declared, "Our children have devoted themselves to the land, and every family has every reason to embrace our soil, to cherish our livestock—horses, cows, pigs, chickens—and our staple crops—corn and wheat." The final segment culminated in a lottery game. The president, temporarily relieved of his duties, yielded the stage to a vice president, who proceeded to announce the winning numbers. Each fortunate recipient was awarded a modest gift—a potted plant, a set of kitchen utensils, or a notebook. Though humble, the recipients accepted their prizes with solemn pride. The climax occurred when Balgen's father emerged as the last winner, receiving a palm-sized notebook graciously presented by his daughter. Their heartfelt exchange of thanks and a handshake elicited applause and laughter from the audience, elevating the atmosphere to unprecedented levels of enthusiasm.

At this juncture, the president signalled the conclusion of the meeting, and dinner commenced. The housewives unveiled their culinary creations, adorning the long dining table with a splendid array of dishes. It was evident that each family had put forth their utmost effort to showcase their culinary prowess at this annual gathering. Intriguingly, there were no duplicate dishes, almost as if everyone had coordinated beforehand. Armed with their own cutlery, attendees eagerly engaged in both eating and lively conversation, exchanging recent experiences. Mrs. Hales's beef stew with potatoes and carrots garnered widespread acclaim, with her clay pot being the first to be emptied. I couldn't help but feel a sense of pride in my earlier prediction; if there were a wager on the evening's most popular dish, I would undoubtedly emerge victorious.

The festivities drew to a close at ten o'clock. Prior to the conclusion, the president returned to the stage and suggested that all attending families turn towards the American flag positioned in the corner of the room and recite an oath. In unison, everyone rose to their feet, placing their hands over their left chests, and solemnly pledged allegiance to the flag, their country, and vowed to uphold truthfulness and loyalty...

This rural gathering, spontaneously orchestrated by a handful of middle school students, may seem modest in its scale, yet its significance for the advancement of American agriculture is difficult to gauge precisely. Nonetheless, it appears that the progress of any cause necessitates the involvement of a dedicated and fervent group of individuals.

Similarly, in the United States, one frequently observes a heightened sense of patriotism in remote locales where ordinary citizens congregate. These communities readily display the national flag at their doorsteps and willingly pledge allegiance to it, even when prompted by a few students.

8

The Red Roof

Little guests in a big cart

Zhang Village is eight li (0.5 kilometres) away from the county town.

Who can truly comprehend the distance of eight li? For adults, it's merely the duration of cooking a meal on foot, or the time it takes to smoke two cigarettes on a bicycle. However, for children around the age of six or seven, it's an entirely different matter: with their little legs taking strides, they would hop and skip, running for quite a stretch, yet they still require the guidance of an adult. Without an adult to lead them, even if they can run, it remains but a fanciful notion.

Take Yuhu and Xiaozhu, for instance: neither has ever had the opportunity to explore beyond the confines of their village. Often, they can be found standing at the village entrance, gazing towards the distant, blurry county town, engaging in lively debates about everything they imagine lies there.

Observing the towering chimney of the cotton ginning factory stretching towards the sky, Xiaozhu turned to Yuhu and inquired, "Do you reckon it's exhaling towards the heavens?"

"What's exhaling? Do you think it's a person? That's just smoke billowing from the chimney!" Yuhu always seemed to express himself vividly compared to Xiaozhu.

"Why is the smoke black for a while and white for a while?"

Now Yuhu couldn't answer. But he knew how to quickly change the topic.

"Forget about the smoke. Just look down the chimney," Yuhu pointed at the distance.

Xiaozhu stood on tiptoe.

"See?" Yuhu asked, holding him by the shoulders.

"Isn't that a tree?"

"Look down."

Xiaozhu stopped talking.

"Don't you see the red houses under the trees?" Finally Yuhu asked.

Xiaozhu let his heels touch the ground

again: "I thought they were red clouds!"

"What red clouds!" Yuhu said with a sense of pride, "Red clouds can't be floating there every day, can they? That's my aunt's school, with red walls and a red roof."

Yuhu thought Xiaozhu would believe him, but Xiaozhu just winked at Yuhu and said, "Hey, where do you see a red roof? The roof of my house is grey, so does your roof, and all the roofs in the village are grey!"

"Only schools have red roofs!" Yuhu explained.

'That's not right either, the roof of school in our village is also grey," Xiaozhu corrected.

"Our village school can't be considered a proper school. There aren't even window panes, and students share the space with pigs. Go and inquire with Big Shengyong from the back street. He attends that school. He'll tell you how many baskets of grass you get when you add two baskets to two baskets," Yuhu retorted.

"Does your aunt know?"

"Of course. My aunt even knows what two hundred baskets plus two hundred baskets is." Yuhu said.

"Big Shengyong is still young."

"He won't know even after a hundred years. And he won't be able to get into university either."

"Can your aunt go to university?"

"Of course."

"Why?"

"Because..." Yuhu thought for a moment and said, "Just because... their school has a red roof."

In reality, Yuhu was well aware of the outcome of his aunt's university entrance exam. She had taken the exam the previous year but had not succeeded, and now she had returned to school to resume her studies. Yuhu was referring to the current year. However, Yuhu's remarks piqued Xiaozhu's curiosity about the red houses. As he squinted and gazed into the distance once more, the crimson clouds he had previously spotted indeed transformed into a collection of red rooftops. Now, Xiaozhu held an even greater admiration for Yuhu.

Yuhu wasn't born knowing that there was a red roof in the city, and the building with the red roof was a school. All of these were told to him by his aunt.

Yuhu's aunt, Xingfen, would return home every week and regale Yuhu with tales from her school. Yuhu not only learned about the red-roofed buildings at her school but also about a quaint red-roofed structure atop one of the buildings—a small bell tower housing the bell that marked the beginning and end of classes. When the bell chimed "dong dong dong," it signaled the commencement of classes, and when it rang again, it signified the conclusion of lessons. This was a departure from the village schools, where whistles were used to indicate class periods. Occasionally, mischievous children who weren't enrolled in school would deliberately blow a whistle outside the school walls, tricking everyone into believing that it was time to end class, leading to chaos as students rushed out of the classrooms. When the teacher blew the whistle to summon them back, the troublemakers would shout from a distance, "The roof is collapsing, the roof is collapsing!" Such antics disrupted the lessons, bringing them to a halt.

Once, Yuhu's aunt gifted him a green school bag, expressing her intention to enroll him in school, much to his dismay. He couldn't help but wonder: Is this what school is really like?

His aunt's school stood apart, distinguished by its red-roofed buildings crowned with a bell tower. The bell held the solemn duty of marking the commencement and conclusion of classes. Even if mischief-makers attempted to disrupt proceedings by blowing a whistle, their efforts would be met with disbelief and disregard.

After gazing at the red roof for a while, Xiaozhu suddenly had a new question: "Yuhu, the house is so mall. Can Auntie Xingfen go into it?"

"The house is not small at all. My aunt said that it looks small from here because we're far away."

"Why does it look small when we're far away?"

"Just because we're far away," Yuhu replied impatiently.

"So far away, can we even get there?" Xiaozhu didn't notice Yuhu's unhappiness.

"My aunt said that if you can see it, you can get there," Yuhu answered.

It was at this moment that a thought suddenly flashed through Yuhu's mind: "Why not go to the town?" As he pondered this, he began pacing back and forth at the entrance of the village, as if waiting for some opportunity.

The opportunity presented itself: Wasn't that Uncle Gao's large cart? Laden with several plump cotton bales, it trundled along the road. As the cart departed from the village entrance, Yuhu swiftly deduced its destination—the cotton ginning factory in town, to deliver the cotton. The prospect of sneaking into the cart ignited a surge of excitement within Yuhu.

Fortunately, as soon as the cart departed the village, Uncle Gao called out "Whoa!" and true to his command, the cart came to a halt. It transpired that he needed to collect a bucket of water to feed the animals, having cast aside his whip. Yuhu gestured to Xiaozhu, who without hesitation, clambered onto the cart from the rear and wedged himself between the cotton bales. Only then did Xiaozhu comprehend the purpose behind Yuhu's earlier aimless wandering at the village entrance. Observing Yuhu's successful manoeuvre, Xiaozhu followed suit, without pausing to consider the repercussions.

In December, nestled among the cotton bales, the warmth and comfort enveloped Yuhu, inducing a drowsy sensation. The eight-li journey seemed to Yuhu like gliding on clouds, while Xiaozhu, on the other hand, felt as though the mountains were swaying and the earth was trembling beneath him.

Aunt is heading back to the village

Yuhu's aunt, Xingfen, and her classmate, Qiaozhen, stood at the entrance of the county middle school, anticipating someone's arrival. Were they waiting for Yuhu? Certainly not, as they were unaware that Yuhu had stealthily hitched a ride amidst the cotton bales and arrived in town. So, whom were they expecting? They were awaiting a passing cart to provide them with a lift back to the village.

Xingfen and Qiaozhen are both from Zhang Village. They both graduated from high school in the summer and neither of them could get into university. Now, they are both attending classes at school again.

As they waited, Xingfen suddenly exclaimed to Qiaozhen, "Look, isn't that Uncle Gao's cart?" As she spoke, the cart had already pulled up in front of them. Uncle Gao reined in the animals and asked, "It's you two, are you heading back to the village?"

"Yes, just waiting for you to give us a ride."

As soon as Xingfen finished speaking, a little boy's head suddenly popped out from the back of the cart, it was Yuhu; then another one popped out right after, no need to ask, this was Xiaozhu.

Yuhu always regarded his aunt's voice as melodious as a radio announcer's. As soon as she "broadcasted" her words, he couldn't contain his excitement and leaped off the cart with a thud, darting towards Xingfen and exclaiming, "Auntie!" Following Yuhu's lead, Xiaozhu also disembarked from the cart and called out, "Auntie!" Xingfen greeted them joyfully, "Oh, I thought the cart was empty, but it turns out you two were aboard. Yuhu, what were you both doing climbing onto the cart?" She reached out to pluck a strand of cotton dangling from Xiaozhu's ear.

Yuhu just smiled and didn't say anything.

Xiaozhu neither smiled nor spoke.

Uncle Gao interjected, "They emerged from the cotton bales while I was unloading them at the cotton gin factory. When I inquired about their presence, one remained silent, and the other mentioned a desire to see the red roof of the county middle school. Now, here they are, but you two are heading back. What's the meaning of this..."

"It's winter vacation. Look at you, so excited about your new cart that you've forgotten the time? You've just graduated a few days ago and already forgotten about the winter vacation."

"Look at me. I'm such an idiot."

"Can we hitch a ride with you? Are you worried about your big mule?"

"Why is it that the more educated you are, the better you get at making sarcastic remarks? Giddy up!" Uncle Gao laughed, and with a shout to urged the animals to move forward.

"Qiaozhen, hurry up and get on!" Xingfen and Qiaozhen quickly picked up their luggage and started loading it onto the cart.

As soon as Xingfen mentioned getting on the cart, Yuhu hurriedly pushed Xiaozhu's back and said, "Look!"

"What?" Xiaozhu had already forgotten

about the red roof.

"What do you think?" Yuhu pointed towards the school gate.

Only then did Xiaozhu suddenly recollect the significance of the red roof. Hastily taking a few strides forward, he pressed against the wall and peered into the courtyard. Ah, before his eyes lay a sea of crimson—red-tiled roofs! The sight of the red roof triggered memories of Xingfen's university entrance exam. Rushing to the front of the cart, he seized Xingfen's arm and queried, "Auntie Xingfen, did you get into university?"

"No, if I had been admitted, would I be standing here waiting for you to call me Auntie?"

Xiaozhu glanced at Yuhu standing next to him, whispering, "You said your aunt could get in, didn't you?"

But Yuhu remained unperturbed. He ruminated, "I was referring to this year. Moreover, I've shown you the red roof. If I hadn't shown you, you might have believed there were no houses with red roofs, mistaking the red roof for red clouds. Now you can see it for yourself. As for my aunt getting into university this year, what's wrong with that? You may not want to be with my aunt, but I do. She tells me so many things."

It was only when Xingfen called out to Yuhu from the cart that Yuhu and Xiaozhu climbed back on the cart.

On the journey, Xingfen engaged in conversation with Uncle Gao, while Qiaozhen remained silent, her expression fraught with concern. Uncle Gao inquired about the margin by which Xingfen fell short of the admission threshold in last year's college entrance examination. Xingfen replied, "Even if I were just one point shy, they still wouldn't have accepted me."

"Xingfen was only three points short, but I was more than thirty points short," Qiaozhen finally spoke.

Xiaozhu thought that no wonder Qiaozhen was always worried.

Uncle Gao whipped the animals. The big mule galloped happily, trotting along at a brisk pace.

Yuhu looked back at the red roof, and it once again looked like a red cloud.

The accident of cigarette roll

Don't assume that just because Yuhu and Xiaozhu went to the town together, they are good friends. Yuhu's original friend was Sanniu from the back street; they had exchanged glass marbles and made promises to each other. But after Sanniu started smoking, Yuhu stopped hanging out with him.

As for Xiaozhu, he finds himself lacking companionship. It's not that he's averse to befriending others, but rather, his peers perceive him as sluggish and show little interest in playing with him, often taunting him with derogatory remarks like "sissy." For instance, during the customary summer pastime of catching crickets on balmy evenings, while others forge ahead, he invariably lags behind, inadvertently treading on their heels. However, when prompted to hasten his pace and run, he struggles to keep up. Just two days ago, Yuhu engaged with Xiaozhu solely out of necessity, unable to find another playmate.

Since Auntie Xingfen returned home, things had taken a different turn. She bestowed upon Yuhu an exercise book—a blue one adorned with green letters. Each day, she would write something in it and then instruct Yuhu to copy it. Phrases like "one, two, three" or "man, hand, knife" (in Chinese characters), or letters like "a, o, c". Consequently, whenever Xiaozhu came looking for Yuhu, he would find him absorbed in his studies, holding up the book and saying, "Can't you see I'm doing my homework?" Xiaozhu was curious to take a peek, but Yuhu would promptly flip the book onto the table and retort, "Look at your hands." Xiaozhu glanced down at his grimy hands, then at Yuhu's pristine exercise book. At that moment, he lost the courage to inquire about Yuhu's homework or to propose going out to play. Instead, he retreated and engaged with Sanniu once more.

Who is Sanniu? Sanniu is a character described as being older than Xiaozhu by only two years, making him nine years old in the current year. Despite his young age, his penchant for smoking may give the impression that he's an adult. However, this habit doesn't deter other children from interacting with him. In fact, Sanniu often finds himself surrounded by a diverse group of children, ranging from those his own age to younger ones still clad in open crotch pants. There are several reasons for his popularity: his family owns the only television in Zhang Village, he possesses a homemade tie and sunglasses which he emulates from television shows, and he owns various toys and props like a toy pistol, a toy dagger with a sheath, sticks, clubs, ropes, and other paraphernalia similar to those owned by the "Gorillas," a group of older boys in the village. When Sanniu takes on the role of "Garrison" and brandishes his toy pistol, his charismatic leadership attracts followers among the children, making him a compelling figure to follow.

Now, when Xiaozhu found Sanniu in the street, Sanniu and a group of children were surrounding a mounting stone and interrogating a "prisoner". The prisoner, a child of four or five years old, was standing on the mounting stone, wailing with tears, but Sanniu was still pointing the gun at him. He aimed the gun at the prisoner's forehead, "Tell me, who sent you? If you say, I'll let you go; if not, I'll execute you on the spot!" After saying this, he pressed the gun against the back of the prisoner's head.

As soon as Xiaozhu saw Sanniu interrogating someone, he ducked his head and tried to blend into the crowd. Seeing the group had grown, Sanniu happily pushed Xiaozhu forward and said, "Fake girl, go and ask who sent him?"

Just as Xiaozhu was hesitating about going forward, an old lady squeezed in from the behind. She slapped Sanniu on the back of his head, shouting, "You naughty boy! All of you, get out of here!"

Seeing that the prisoner now had a backer, Sanniu waved his arm and said, "Xiaozhu, let's go, time for drills!" Then, he led the group running down the street like a swarm of bees.

Among the group of children, Sanniu invited Xiaozhu to join him in the drills, which filled Xiaozhu with joy. This time, he found a newfound energy and ran closely behind Sanniu. When Sanniu was the first to reach the summit of the mound at the village entrance, Xiaozhu closely followed as the second. However, the moment he ascended the mound, he immediately became Sanniu's target. Sanniu playfully nudged Xiaozhu's hat with his toy pistol, loosened the tie around his neck, and teasingly said, "Zhu, hand it over!"

"What...what do you want me to take?" Xiaozhu asked, puzzled.

"Don't play dumb, give back my stuff!" Sanniu took another step forward.

"What stuff?" Xiaozhu asked.

"You are forgetful, huh? Let me remind you," Sanniu said, forming a circle with his thumb and index finger, blowing on them, and then flicking Xiaozhu's forehead. Xiaozhu covered his head and turned to run, but Sanniu blocked his way and said, "If you can't pay back cigarettes, you can give something else!"

As soon as Sanniu mentioned the cigarette, Xiaozhu's memory was jogged. A few days prior, Sanniu's mother had caught him smoking and pursued him down the street, aiming to reprimand him. In his panicked flight, Sanniu had encountered Xiaozhu approaching, and without hesitation, he thrust half a cigarette into Xiaozhu's pocket. Upon noticing the half cigarette, Xiaozhu acted swiftly, joining Sanniu in his escape. However, when Sanniu eventually eluded his mother's pursuit and sought the cigarette from Xiaozhu, it was nowhere to be found. It transpired that there was a hole in Xiaozhu's pocket, and the cigarette had slipped out somewhere along the way. Thus, Xiaozhu found himself indebted to Sanniu for half a cigarette. Henceforth, whenever Sanniu sought confrontation with Xiaozhu, he would demand the owed cigarette.

This incident had occurred quite some time ago, and Xiaozhu assumed that Sanniu had let it go. However, to his surprise, Sanniu still harboured resentment. He seized Xiaozhu by the collar, causing Xiaozhu to attempt to retreat, but Sanniu's grip only tightened, preventing any escape. Xiaozhu attempted to twist away, managing to turn halfway, yet Sanniu persisted, dragging him in a full circle. Just then, Xiaozhu's mother came running, shouting as she approached. Sensing the escalating tension, Sanniu released Xiaozhu and swiftly vanished from sight. Left behind were Xiaozhu, his mother, and a group of women who had gathered at the base of the mound.

Xiaozhu's mother, leaning on a shovel, admonished, "Look at you, always so idle, yet never missing an opportunity to stir up trouble. When you disappeared into town on that cart, I spent half the day searching for you. And now, what mischief have you managed to get into today?" Casting her gaze around, she spotted Xingfen, as if finding a witness to her son's antics. She seized Xingfen's arm and implored, "See, Xingfen is here. She witnessed what happened in town that day. Let Xingfen tell you, can you carry on like this?"

As Xiaozhu's mother grasped Xingfen's arm, Xiaozhu also seized her other arm, casting pleading glances in her direction, hoping she would intercede on his behalf. However, after a brief pause, Xingfen addressed Xiaozhu with a hint of irritation, "Honestly, how can you continue to behave like this?" Yet, despite her admonishment, she couldn't suppress a chuckle.

As Xingfen laughed, Xiaozhu felt a bit relaxed.

"Tell Auntie, what happened today?" Xingfen asked Xiaozhu.

"Sanniu asked me for something," Xiaozhu said with his head down.

"Ah, you owe him something!" Xiaozhu's mother burst into fury upon hearing this.

Xingfen quickly asked Xiaozhu, "Zhu, what do you owe him?"

"Half a cigarette," Xiaozhu replied, peeking at his mother's expression.

"What?" Xiaozhu's mother reacted as if she had been stung by a wasp, "My little rascal, are you still smoking?" As she shouted, she reached out to scratch Xiaozhu.

Fortunately, Xingfen and a few aunts held back Xiaozhu's mother. Xiaozhu quickly explained, "I don't smoke. It's Sanniu."

"Then why is he asking you for cigarette?" Xingfen asked. "Does this kid deserve a beating or not?" Xiaozhu's mother was about to grab Xiaozhu's arm again.

Xingfen turned to Xiaozhu's mother and said, "He deserves a beating. He deserves a beating!" But then she whispered to Xiaozhu, "Run, quick!"

Only then did Xiaozhu squeeze out of the crowd, took a few steps back, ran down the mound, and sprinted off into the distance.

Xiaozhu's mother looked at Xingfen helplessly and said, "Ah, you are such a..."

Xingfen smiled and said, "Aunt, if you use up all your energy now, how will you work? Are you not going to the farm?"

Xingfen's words elicited laughter from everyone present. Eventually, the laughter subsided, and the group escorted Xiaozhu's mother back home. Several children clad in open-crotch pants were also led away by their parents. Throughout the journey, Xiaozhu's mother engaged in conversation with those accompanying her, expressing her concerns, "The school won't accept him, and neither will the nursery centre. With our hands full tending to the farm, managing everything at home becomes quite a challenge."

"That's true," the people agreed.

The street was now empty except for Yuhu, who had witnessed everything that had just happened.

Accident

Yuhu learned that Xiaozhu's mother was upset with him, not only due to Sanniu's demand for a cigarette but also because of their trip to town. Feeling despondent upon returning home, Yuhu pondered over the situation. He believed that while Xiaozhu often caused trouble for his mother, the blame for their excursion to town couldn't be solely attributed to him. Furthermore, if Xiaozhu's mother knew the true reason behind their trip, perhaps she wouldn't be so angry. Regarding the cigarette incident, Yuhu was fully aware of the circumstances—it was entirely Sanniu's fault. Determined to rectify the misunderstanding, Yuhu contemplated going to explain everything to Xiaozhu's mother.

The next morning, he mustered his courage and went to Xiaozhu's house alone.

The courtyard of Xiaozhu's house lay deserted, save for an ancient jujube tree. A flock of sparrows chattered amidst its branches, taking flight in unison as someone approached, alighting upon the rooftop with a flurry of wings. Yuhu ascended the steps and noticed a sizable iron lock adorning the door, surmising that his mother must have gone to grind. Where was Xiaozhu? Perhaps he had forgotten about their altercation and gone off to play with Sanniu again. Just as Yuhu contemplated leaving, he heard his name being called from behind—a voice eerily reminiscent of Xiaozhu's. Turning around, he scanned the courtyard, yet found it empty. About to depart once more, he was startled by another call from behind, "Yuhu, I'm here, inside the house!"

Upon hearing the voice, Yuhu realised it was indeed Xiaozhu. He run to the window and saw a small head inside the small glass pane, which was Xiaozhu. Yuhu immediately understood what was going on.

Xiaozhu knocked on the window and asked, "Yuhu, can you open it for me?"

Yuhu thought: You deserve to be locked up for always hanging out with Sanniu! But then he reconsidered: What am I here for? Can I just ignore this?

"Where's the key?" Yuhu asked Xiaozhu through the glass.

"Hanging on top of the door frame," Xiaozhu said, nudging the window glass with his nose.

Yuhu ran to the door, looked up, and saw

a key sticking out from the top of the door frame. He tried to reach it on his tiptoes, but it was still too high. He thought about stacking some bricks to stand on. Just then, a group of people ran in through the fence gate, with Sanniu leading the way.

As soon as Yuhu saw Sanniu, he pulled a long face and said, "It's all your fault for asking him for cigarettes. Look at this!" He pointed towards the house.

"And you, taking him to the town," Sanniu retorted.

Yuhu was about to argue with Sanniu: How could asking for cigarettes be the same as taking someone to the town? But seeing Sanniu and his gang holding sticks and staring at him menacingly, he hesitated for a moment, and then quickly walked away.

As soon as Yuhu left, Sanniu started

making sarcastic remarks behind him: "Not helping a friend in need, that's not a good friend." Then, He said to Xiaozhu, "Wait, Garrison will let you out!"

It appeared that Yuhu was aware of Xiaozhu's confinement and arrived to rescue him. He directed a kid named Erxing to crouch down, then stepped onto Erxing's shoulders. With determination, Erxing clenched his fists and rose, allowing Sanniu to effortlessly reach the key. Without waiting for Erxing to squat down again, Sanniu leaped off his shoulders and passed the key to Erxing to unlock the door. Erxing was known as the specialist in unlocking among their group, dubbed the "Gorillas."

Xiaozhu hesitantly walked out of the house, looked at Sanniu and then at Yuhu, and said, "Sanniu, let's play something good.

I don't want to do anything that will get me scolded again."

Sanniu said nonchalantly, "Of course, let's play something interesting. What do you want to play?"

"Let's... let's play classes," Xiaozhu saw Yuhu and remembered the red roof.

"Alright, let's do class role play," Sanniu agreed with a wave of his hand.

A group of children swarmed around him and immediately started shouting, "It's time for class!"

"Who will be the teacher?" a child asked Sanniu.

"You guys choose," Sanniu said generously to everyone.

After hearing that, the children all clamored and shouted, "I'll be the teacher, me!"

"I have chalks!"

"I can read!"

"Stop, I'll be the teacher!" In fact, Sanniu was waiting to be chosen. But when he saw that no one was nominating him, he suddenly changed his mind.

"Dabao, give me your chalk!" Sanniu shouted to a child wearing open-crotch pants.

Dabao didn't dare to disobey the order and handed the chalk to Sanniu obediently.

Holding the chalk, Sanniu walked up to the dark grey wall of Xiaozhu's house and said in a strange tone, "Sit down, everyone. I can do arithmetic! Now, I'll teach you."

Everyone sat down in a small area.

"Look, I'm going to do some math! What's this?" He wrote a "4" on the wall with the chalk.

The children all stared at the wall without

saying a word.

Sanniu started to be impatient: "Why aren't you talking? I'm going to choose someone. Li Xiaozhu, stand up!"

Xiaozhu followed the order. He didn't recognize the character on the wall, so he didn't dare to look straight ahead, only glancing at the sky and the ground from time to time.

"Speak up!" Sanniu glared.

Xiaozhu quickly closed his eyes and said, "It's 5!"

"Alright, let's say it's 5. What's this?" Sanniu wrote another "2" on the wall.

Xiaozhu answered without hesitation, "This one is 3."

"You got it right again. What's the total?" Sanniu put on his glasses and looked at Xiaozhu from the side of them, pretending to be a teacher.

This really stumped Xiaozhu.

"Let me tell you, it's 9!" Sanniu said, waving his hand.

But Xiaozhu seemed to doubt Sanniu's answer. He counted on his fingers and said, "No, it's 7."

"It's 9!" Sanniu took off his glasses, clearly annoyed.

At that moment, Yuhu, who had been standing at the rear observing the lesson, couldn't contain himself any longer. He exclaimed, "That's not true!" It transpired that he had been on the verge of departing when he overheard the enactment of teacher and student roles. Intrigued, he paused and positioned himself at the back to observe the game.

Seeing Yuhu interrupt, Sanniu pulled

out his toy gun from his waist and pointed it towards the sky, saying, "Nonsense. Arrest him!"

"Stop!"

"Hands up!"

Those children shouted, grabbing sticks around them and swarming towards Yuhu. Those who couldn't get close waved their small fists in the air and followed the commotion.

Yuhu took a few steps backward, then pushed his cotton hat to the back of his head. He had been harboring a desire to confront Sanniu for some time. Whether or not he could best Sanniu in a fight was irrelevant; what mattered was asserting himself and showing Sanniu that he wasn't someone to be underestimated. Yuhu was determined to make Sanniu realize that a worn-out cloth around the neck, a fractured bamboo piece tucked into the waist, and those paper-cut black glasses that offered no real vision couldn't intimidate anyone.

Just as Yuhu was about to lunge forward, Xingfen suddenly appeared in front of them. She first hugged Yuhu around his waist, then looked at the situation in the courtyard and said kindly, "You're role-playing, right? How about I be your teacher for a while?"

Upon learning that Auntie Xingfen expressed her desire to be their teacher, a sense of astonishment swept through the group, prompting puzzled glances exchanged among them. What could this mean? After all, wasn't she just a high school student? With her fair and pretty appearance, why would she want to engage with them? Despite these uncertainties, a few of the younger children rushed forward eagerly, seizing Aunt Xingfen's hand with enthusiasm.

Sanniu stood aside, being silent and skeptical.

Yuhu opposed his aunt's decision vehemently. He attempted to pull Xingfen away by grabbing her arm, but Xingfen resisted and pulled Yuhu back. With a nonchalant demeanor, she plucked a stalk of sorghum from the bundle of firewood in the corner, gestured towards the wall in front of the children, and remarked, "I've been observing you from the doorway for some time. If you aspire to be a student, you must learn to write characters correctly. Your current approach to reading and writing is flawed. How do you expect to be students if you're merely scribbling and mumbling?"

"How could it be wrong?" someone asked from behind.

"It's not quite right," Xingfen remarked, pointing at the "4" depicted on the wall with the stalk. "Let's begin with this. It's not pronounced as 5; it's actually 4, but you need to turn it around like this." She retrieved a piece of chalk from the ground and proceeded to inscribe a correct "4" on the wall. "Now, let's address this one. It's pronounced as 2, not 3, but it should be standing upright, like so." With precision, Xingfen illustrated the proper form of the number "2" on the wall. "See, it resembles a little duck swimming. Now, what is 4 plus 2? Allow me to demonstrate." With that, Xingfen inscribed the equation "4+2" on the wall.

Just as Xingfen was about to proceed, a child with a prominent belt hurried up to Sanniu and whispered something into his ear. Sanniu brandished his toy gun and proclaimed, "There's a new development! Those unafraid of facing death, come with me!" With a swift motion, he swung his arm and dashed outside. The other children followed him in a swarm.

Xingfen turned her head and noticed that only Yuhu and a small girl remained in the yard. Yuhu seemed oblivious to the presence of the little girl; he regarded his aunt with sympathy and remarked, "I attempted to persuade you to leave, but you were determined to teach. And now, they've all scattered, haven't they?"

"But there are still people here, aren't there?" Xingfen pointed to the little girl.

Only then, did Yuhu notice that there was someone behind him. She had a pale face, yellow hair, and a small, crooked pigtail. Wasn't this Xiuxiu?

Although Xiuxiu still stayed at Zhang Village, she wasn't born here. It is her grandmother that lived next door to Yuhu's house in Zhang Village. But what use was there in her staying behind? He spoke to Xiuxiu with a bit of irritation, "Why didn't you run with Sanniu?"

"I don't want to go with Sanniu. I want to know what 4 plus 2 is," Xiuxiu replied.

"What's the use in knowing that, you're not from Zhang Village," Yuhu said.

As soon as Yuhu mentioned that Xiuxiu wasn't from Zhang Village, she was at a loss for words.

"Do you really want to know what 4 plus 2 is?" Xingfen quickly ran over and bent down to ask Xiuxiu.

"Yes, I do," Xiuxiu answered confidently.

"Then don't worry. I'll definitely teach

you. Not only will I teach you 4 plus 2, but I'll teach you other things too," Xingfen said.

"How can Aunt Xingfen teach you if you leave?" Yuhu asked.

"My mum said that this time she brought me to my grandma's house, we're not going back," Xiuxiu replied.

"Why aren't you going back?"

As Xingfen asked, Xiuxiu lowered her head and stopped talking.

New situation

The recent development that's just come to light occurred at the nursery center in the eastern part of the village, where the director happens to be the elderly lady who reprimanded Sanniu as a "naughty boy" a couple of days ago. She's a beneficiary of the Five-Guarantee system, and she's affectionately known as "Grandma Wubao (Five Guarantees)" by everyone.

Grandma Wubao observed that following the introduction of the household responsibility system in the village, numerous families found themselves unable to tend to farm duties due to childcare responsibilities. Consequently, she approached the village party secretary, Grandpa Wugeng, with the proposition of establishing a nursery. Initially, the nursery received warm reception from the villagers. However, before long, the number of children attending dwindled. What could be the cause? It transpired that many had joined Sanniu's "Gorillas". Those who refrained from joining were coerced by Sanniu himself, who would venture to the nursery to "rescue" them, likening it to liberating orphans from an orphanage. Children who had joined the "Gorillas" and returned to the nursery faced even graver repercussions. But why didn't the adults intervene? They harbored apprehensions, not towards Sanniu, but his brother, who served as a driver for the commune secretary.

The "prisoner" that Sanniu captured in the street was a boy from the nursery, named Stinky. Someone caught him returned to the nursery after being a "prisoner" and reported it to Sanniu.

Sanniu lead his group and ran straight to the nursery from Xiaozhu's house. He stepped on a child's shoulder to climb over the wall.

There was no one in the yard.

After inserting a match head into his gun, he pulled the trigger, and it discharged with a bang. Then, he called out towards the yard, "Everyone, come out! Stand up! Don't be afraid. We're here to save you!" The yard remained quiet and motionless. Impatiently, Sanniu turned to Xiaozhu and remarked, "Zhu, search the house. Once you apprehend Stinky, then we're in the clear."

Upon learning that Sanniu had granted him an opportunity for redemption, Xiaozhu stooped down, protruded his buttocks, and began to inch his way toward the door. Witnessing Xiaozhu taking the initiative, the other children trailed behind. However, as they approached the door, the curtain was abruptly drawn aside, unveiling Grandma Wubao. Spotting her, Xiaozhu swiftly retreated. Granny cried out, "Halt! Detain me! Detain me! I am the sole remaining one, simply take me away!"

"We don't want you. We despise you because you have bound feet!" Sanniu shouted from atop the wall.

"We want Stink!" Seeing Sanniu's boldness, Xiaozhu also chimed in with a shout.

"You've scared him away long ago!" Grandma Wubao quivered with anger.

Was Stink really scared away? No. He was hiding in the house with a few younger children. They were huddled together on the kang (a traditional Chinese heated bed), not daring to make a sound.

At that moment, Xingfen entered the yard, followed by Yuhu. They were following from Xiaozhu's house. As soon as Xiaozhu saw Xingfen, he scurried along the wall and ran out of the yard. After Xiaozhu left the yard, Sanniu also jumped off the wall and ran into the street.

As soon as Grandma Wubao saw Xingfen, she clapped her hands and exclaimed, "Xingfen, look! They'll be coming to arrest me next!"

Xingfen laughed and said, "Grandma, it'll definitely be your turn next time."

"You're still laughing, and you're not even standing up for me," Granny Wu Bao retorted.

"I really want to help you," Xingfen said earnestly.

How could Auntie Xingfen stand up for Grandma Wubao? Yuhu didn't understand. He followed his aunt out of the nursery and ran into Qiaozhen at the street corner. Qiaozhen was not only Xingfen's classmate but also Sanniu's sister. She had come to the street to look for Sanniu.

"Have you seen Sanniu?" Qiaozhen asked Yuhu.

Yuhu looked at his aunt but remained silent.

"I saw him," Xingfen said, "He was just there with a gun, trying to catch someone."

"He always makes people complain to my parents, which really affects our relationships with others," Qiaozhen said.

"He is also smoking," Xingfen added.

"What can we do?" Qiaozhen looked at Xingfen, seeking advice.

"Let's think of a way to handle this," Xingfen said, looking at Qiaozhen.

"What's the solution?"

"Can't we try to educate them?"

"Ah, you're not going to the tutoring class?"

"Let's take care of them first."

"I don't have that kind of patience. Besides, my dad bought me a knitting machine, and I can earn quite a bit by knitting a sweater."

"So you're not going to the tutoring class?" Xingfen asked Qiaozhen again.

"Anyway, I lack confidence in getting into university. You're different from me; don't be half-hearted about your university entrance exam, or it would be such a pity."

Qiaozhen didn't pay much attention to Xingfen's words. She left Xingfen and Yuhu behind and turned to another street to look for Sanniu.

Yuhu remained perplexed, querying as they strolled, "How are we going to educate them? How are we going to take care of this?" His aunt simply walked with her head bowed, as if she hadn't heard him. It wasn't until the evening that Yuhu comprehended what his aunt had meant.

Schoolbags with zippers

After dinner, Xingfen was washing dishes by the sink when Grandpa Wugeng came by.

Grandpa Wugeng sat down on a small cabinet after entering the room, and said to Auntie Xingfen, "Xingfen, I heard that last time you were only three points short of entering a college?"

" If I were just one point short, they wouldn't take me either," Auntie Xingfen replied with her usual line.

"Let's see what happens this year. I just can't believe that our Zhang Village can't develop a few promising individuals. Even if there are no university students, vocational school students can still make us happy. Our village was weak in infrastructure. Everyone was so poor that no one had the time to focus on the educational development."

Yuhu was reclining on the edge of the kang, folding paper aeroplanes. However, as soon as he caught wind of Grandpa Wugeng and Auntie Xingfen discussing schools, he abandoned the aeroplane and edged closer to the shaft of light to eavesdrop. He overheard Auntie Xingfen echoing what Grandpa Wugeng had said, "Now we've finally recovered from the ordeal."

"These past two years, we've become richer. But people are still working from dawn to dusk, education hasn't been given much attention. Look at the chaos all day long," said Grandpa Wugeng, as he filled his pipe with tobacco.

"The hustle and bustle saves us the trouble

of inviting a drama troupe," Auntie Xingfen said after washing the dishes and sitting down on the edge of the kang.

Yuhu felt disheartened: What's happening with Auntie? She was discussing taking action against Sanniu's mischief during the day, but now she seems to think it's easier than inviting a drama troupe. Does she find the chaos and altercations more entertaining than the performances of the county drama troupe? He wanted to voice his thoughts but feared Auntie might scold him away, so he remained silent in the shadows, holding his breath. He glanced at Grandpa Wugeng, who was puffing on his pipe with a troubled expression. Grandpa Wugeng remarked, "The more chaos I witness, the more incensed I become. Every time I see those children running around the streets, I feel remorseful. Is there no one willing to take charge?" Yuhu thought Grandpa Wugeng's words were sensible.

"Grandpa Wugeng, are you using reverse psychology on me?" Auntie Xingfen asked with a smile.

"Whether I'm using reverse psychology or not, I can't allow it to affect your future," Grandpa Wugeng replied.

"What if I'm willing to do?"

"Speak up a bit louder. My hearing isn't as sharp as it used to be."

In fact, Grandpa Wugeng's hearing was not at all bad. But for some reason, Yuhu also wanted to hear Auntie Xingfen say it again.

"What if I'm willing to do?" Auntie Xingfen repeated.

"What about the college entrance examination?" Grandpa Wugeng asked.

"Let's take care of this first. When it comes

to the college entrance exam this year, we can have someone replace me," Auntie Xingfen replied.

"Xingfen, if it weren't for you saying, I wouldn't have the heart to bother you. But I heard that you teach the children, and I was so happy that I didn't enjoy my lunch well. What's your plan for them in the future?"

"Let's start a preschool class to teach the children some knowledge. It's always better than having them run around the streets with knives and guns, cursing and fighting," Auntie Xingfen suggested.

Ah, it transpired that Auntie's initial words weren't genuine; her true intention was to establish a school, with herself as the teacher. Yuhu gazed at Auntie, noticing that she appeared more radiant than ever. Beneath the light, her lips gleamed like crimson velvet.

With a teacher like Auntie, what couldn't one learn? But where would the school be located? In the red-roofed building? Would there be a substantial bell? Would Grandpa Wugeng approve? Yuhu pondered these questions, feeling so exhilarated that he nearly applauded, but he refrained: what if they caught him eavesdropping and ceased their conversation? He listened attentively. Grandpa Wugeng remarked, "You see, it's because you're educated."

"It's not that I'm educated, and the idea for the preschool class isn't my idea. I saw it in a pictorial magazine," Auntie Xingfen explained.

"This is a good idea," Grandpa Wugeng agreed.

Yuhu finally felt relieved.

"Education has to start from a young age," Auntie Xingfen added.

"It's like farming. The plan for the year is made in spring, and the plan for the day is made in the morning," Grandpa Wugeng said.

Auntie Xingfen and Grandpa Wugeng reached a consensus that the preschool class would exclusively admit children aged five to eight years old. They also deliberated on the registration procedure, who would oversee the renovation of the building, and the arrangements for preparing tables and desks. They meticulously addressed every aspect of the plan before Grandpa Wugeng departed from the house.

As soon as Grandpa Wugeng left, Yuhu sprang out from the shadows, hugged Auntie Xingfen's waist, and said, "Auntie, let me call you Miss Zhang first!"

Auntie Xingfen replied, "Save it for the day school starts. For now, you still have to call me Auntie."

Yuhu let go of Xingfen and said, "No, I want to call you Miss Zhang! Miss Zhang! Miss Zhang!"

Yuhu called out three times loudly, and it was only after the third time that Auntie Xingfen softly responded with a "Yes".

The following morning, as soon as Yuhu awoke, he recalled the discussion between Auntie and Grandpa Wugeng. He leapt out of bed, snatched his cotton jacket, and dashed outside, eager to share the news with his acquaintances. However, as soon as he stepped beyond the threshold, he pondered, who are my companions? Should I inform Xiaozhu first? No, Xiaozhu couldn't be considered a companion; he might disclose it to Sanniu as soon as he learns. If Sanniu brings his gang to school, it would be disastrous. Contemplating this, Yuhu slowed his pace. As he ambled, he considered mentioning it to some other individuals but felt it wasn't the opportune moment. Eventually, for some inexplicable reason, he suddenly thought of the little girl with a dog-tail plait—Xiuxiu. She resides next door, doesn't she?

Yuhu went into Xiuxiu's grandmother's abode. Xiuxiu was clutching a small basket, assisting her grandmother in feeding the chickens. The moment she spotted Yuhu entering the yard, she set down the basket and hurried over to him, inquiring, "Are you seeking me?"

"Yes!"

"What's wrong?"

"You have to come with me to the south of the village, and then I'll tell you what's going on," Yuhu said, thinking that secrets should be shared in a secret place.

Upon hearing Yuhu's proposal to escort her to the southern part of the village, Xiuxiu became so elated that she abandoned her task of feeding the chickens. Placing the basket on the steps, she promptly followed Yuhu without any hesitation. Yuhu took the lead, with Xiuxiu trailing behind, as the two dashed along a golden dirt track, all the way to the sandy ridge situated in the southern reaches of the village.

There stood a willow forest atop the sandy ridge, its trees clustered densely. The moment the duo entered the forest, Xiuxiu lost sight of Yuhu. She navigated through the trees, calling out for him. She only caught fragments of his voice carried by the wind, but his form eluded her. Xiuxiu felt tears welling up, and then suddenly, Yuhu emerged, intercepting her.

"Why are you just running and not saying anything?" Xiuxiu asked, her voice trembling, "Now you can tell me, right?"

"What's behind you?"

Xiuxiu turned around to look, and Yuhu disappeared again.

"Yuhu, where are you?" Xiuxiu called out softly.

"Am I right in front of you?"

Yuhu slid down from the tree.

"I'm leaving!" Xiuxiu pouted.

As soon as Xiuxiu mentioned leaving, Yuhu became anxious. He said to her, "Xiuxiu, let's guess riddles."

"Do we need to come here to guess riddles?"

"Listen to this riddle—A group of geese came from the south and splashed into the river. Do you know what it is?"

"Dumplings! You think I don't know, huh?"

"Let me tell you another one."

"Whatever you say, I can guess it."

"With a round belly, chubby and plump, it eats notebooks and books alike. Can you guess what it is?"

"A drawer."

"No, that's not right. A drawer cant be chubby."

"A baggage. A baggage is chubby."

"Does a baggage eat books?"

Xiuxiu couldn't come up with an answer, so she tilted her head back and stared at the willow trees.

"Think carefully. What do students carry on their shoulders when they go to school?"

"A schoolbag, of course! Ah, a schoolbag!" Xiuxiu clapped her hands.

"Do you have one?"

"I don't have one. What would I need a schoolbag for?"

"Prepare one soon," Yuhu said seriously.

Xiuxiu wasn't slow-witted; she immediately remembered what Auntie Xingfen had told her that day. "Is it about going to school?" she asked Yuhu excitedly.

"Yes, it's about going to school," Yuhu nodded.

"Is Sanniu the teacher?"

"He's not even qualified to be a student, let alone a teacher."

"Who will be the teacher?"

"My aunt."

"I guessed right."

"But you just guessed it was Sanniu."

"I was afraid it might be Sanniu. Do you have a schoolbag?" Xiuxiu asked Yuhu with concern.

"I do. Do you want to see it?"

"I'd love to. I'll tell my mum what it looks like when I get home. She loves me the most," Xiuxiu said.

Before Xiuxiu could complete her sentence, Yuhu seized her hand, and they sprinted back home. They dashed through the willow forest, descended the sandy ridge, took a shortcut by clambering over a half-wall, and entered the house without traversing the street door. Yuhu stepped onto a small cabinet, lifted the lid of a large chest, and brandished a brand-new, green schoolbag, displaying it to Xiuxiu.

"Oh, it's so green!" Xiuxiu exclaimed as soon as she saw it.

"Look, it has a square belly," Yuhu said.

"That's not chubby."

"How about filling it with books?"

Xiuxiu got it.

"Take a look at the back," Yuhu said, flipping the schoolbag over.

It turned out that there was a silver zipper on the back of the school bag.

"Let's go, let's find your aunt," Xiuxiu said, helping Yuhu put the schoolbag on his shoulder.

"Not yet. We have to wait until the house has a red roof and the bird chirps. Then we'll go to school with our schoolbags," Yuhu said with a smile.

A green jeep

Just after the New Year, before the willow trees had even begun to sprout green leaves, the birds had already sung their cheerful melodies of "Chacha chacha chacha—doo-er!" The word of Auntie Xingfen initiating a preschool in Zhang Village had already circulated far and wide.

Uncle Gao, accompanied by a few league members, was diligently plastering the ceiling and walls. However, they hadn't yet installed a red roof on the building, as the school was repurposed from an old house. Grandpa Wugeng and Auntie Xingfen had reached out to the commune's brick and tile factory, hoping to replace the old roof with vibrant red tiles. Regrettably, they were informed of a tile shortage owing to the heightened demand for tile-roofed houses over the past two years. They would need to join a waiting list to procure them, with no specific date provided for when they could expect delivery.

This situation left Yuhu feeling perpetually disheartened.

When the school construction started, he and Xiuxiu were active in mixing mud and applying plaster. But after hearing that the school wouldn't have a red roof, they couldn't pick up their spirits.

One day, Yuhu and Xiuxiu were walking home listlessly when they accidentally bumped into Xiaozhu. Yuhu hadn't seen Xiaozhu for a long time because Sanniu didn't allow Xiaozhu to come to this street. Why? It was because the school was being built on this street. Sanniu had warned that if Xiaozhu ever went near the school, he would never see Sanniu again.

Today, Xiaozhu sneaked here along the wall, facing the risk of being caught, to meet Yuhu. Why did he want to meet Yuhu? Because he had something to tell him, something that Sanniu had told him. Even though Sanniu had repeatedly instructed Xiaozhu to keep it secretly, Xiaozhu couldn't hold it any more.

Xiaozhu was walking cautiously along the street, trying to avoid being caught, when he ran into Yuhu. However, it seemed as if Yuhu didn't notice him at all. Xiaozhu wasn't sure whether Yuhu really didn't see him or was just pretending. Xiaozhu thought that compared to Sanniu, Yuhu was much better in every way. But there was one demerit of Yuhu: he seemed to look down on others. There was a living person standing right in front of him, and Yuhu didn't share a glance. It was the little girl behind Yuhu who called out to Xiaozhu first.

The little girl is Xiuxiu. Although they didn't live on the same street, Xiaozhu recognised her as the one who was also in the role plays in his courtyard. When Xiuxiu called out to Xiaozhu, she looked back at Yuhu, hoping that he would stop and say something to Xiaozhu. But Yuhu didn't turn around. Feeling a little bit guilty, Xiuxiu quickly grabbed Yuhu's arm and said, "He's looking for you!"

"How do you know?" Yuhu questioned Xiuxiu, continuing to walk forward.

"Yuhu, I really am looking for you," Xiaozhu said anxiously, quickly catching up with a couple of steps.

Seeing Xiaozhu catching up, Yuhu finally stopped.

"Yuhu, are you going to school?" Xiaozhu asked nervously.

"Yes."

"But Sanniu said your school won't be able

to open," Xiaozhu said.

"Do you think we won't open the school just because there's no red roof?" Yuhu thought to himself, suspecting that this must be another rumour spread by Sanniu. Even if the school didn't have a red roof and he was unhappy about it, he couldn't show these in front of them. Besides, now it doesn't have red roof, it doesn't mean that it would never have one in the future.

"Yes, how can you go to school without a red roof?" Xiaozhu said earnestly, then he pointed at Xiuxiu, "Big Horse Face is here. Yep, it's Xiuxiu's father! He won't give you the red tiles and is arguing with Auntie Xingfen at the brigade office."

Yuhu was aware that Xiuxiu's father was known as Big Horse Face and held the position of a procurement officer at the commune's brick and tile factory. He recalled that Grandpa Wugeng had visited the factory to seek him out previously. Given the shortage of red tiles, Yuhu couldn't understand why Grandpa Wugeng would be arguing with Auntie Xingfen. The situation puzzled him greatly.

Xiaozhu looked at Xiuxiu and then at Yuhu, thinking that although Sanniu loved to lie, this time he was telling the truth. Xiaozhu quickly said to Yuhu, "If you don't believe me, I'll take you to the brigade headquarters to see by yourself. There's even a small jeep parked at the entrance!"

Yuhu's impatience got the better of him. He left Xiaozhu and Xiuxiu behind and dashed towards the brigade headquarters. Xiuxiu was on the verge of chasing after Yuhu, but then she hesitated, considering the possibility that Xiaozhu's words might hold some truth. She stood in the street, deep in contemplation.

Xiaozhu felt relieved that Xiuxiu didn't pursue Yuhu. He understood that without Yuhu around, he could expect a much warmer reception from Xiuxiu. Feeling a rush of satisfaction, he abruptly turned to Xiuxiu and uttered rudely, "Hurry up and head home! When the little jeep revs up, it goes zoom zoom zoom!" With that remark, he shook his head and trotted off with a self-satisfied smirk.

Yuhu sprinted all the way to the brigade headquarters' entrance, anticipating to spot a small jeep initially. However, there was nothing there. He thought to himself, "How did I fall for this again!" He then dashed into the courtyard, only to find no jeep there either. As he glanced at the doors, he noticed they were locked. Disheartened, he made his way back home.

The moment Yuhu stepped into the house, he laid eyes on a figure seated on a chair engaged in conversation with his aunt. The man had an elongated face, resembling that of a horse. Big Horse Face didn't acknowledge Yuhu's presence, continuing to chat with his aunt with a smile.

"Xingfen, I got a bit emotional back at the brigade headquarters. I understand your determination to run the school. Seeing the children without a place to study, how can I not worry? But our factory simply can't solve the problem. I went out of my way to contact a brick factory in the neighboring town to get you a batch of tiles, each costing just an extra five cents. I hurried here to share this good news with you, but you still think it's too expensive. If you want to run a school, can you afford to be afraid of spending money?"

"But we also need to spend our money wisely. How can the same red tiles be so much more expensive?"

"Don't you trust me?... In my opinion, no matter how much it costs, we should have a red roof. It's for the younger generation," Big Horse Face said, casting a glance at Yuhu.

"Can't our factory really spare the tiles for a classroom?"

"Indeed, we can't."

"But I saw Sanniu's brother hauling a cart of red tiles home yesterday," Auntie Xingfen's voice rose a little bit.

"He had already ordered them in advance," Big Horse Face paused, his tone tinged with irritation. "Forget it, forget it. You're skeptical, but I'm sincere. If the deal doesn't go through, at least the goodwill is genuine. I don't have many tricks up my sleeve... If you're patient, you can wait for the cheaper one."

"That's right," Auntie Xingfen replied decisively.

Big Horse Face stood up, and as he was about to leave, he patted Yuhu on the head. Yuhu turned his neck slightly, thinking to himself: So you are Xiuxiu's father. Please don't pat her head again.

As soon as Big Horse Face left, Yuhu quickly asked Xingfen, "He said he could bring red tiles from a neighbouring town for us, why did you not want them?"

"You talk nicely, but it's all for personal gain," Auntie Xingfen said with a stern look.

"What does 'profit from it' mean?"

"It means... I can't explain it clearly to you. Do you know about speculation and profiteering?..."

Before Aunt Xingfen could finish speaking, a commotion erupted from the other side of the wall. Yuhu dashed into the yard, climbed onto the chicken coop, and peered over the half wall into Xiuxiu's grandmother's courtyard. His attention was immediately drawn to a green object: was that a green jeep? He had glimpsed similar green vehicles several times on the highway to the south of the village, but they always sped by too quickly to examine closely. Now, he could clearly see that the green top was made of cloth. There were two lamps at the front, and a round wheel was mounted in the front window glass.

He scrutinized the scene and discerned a figure seated behind the circular wheel. The man was lounging in his seat, puffing on a cigarette while wearing a pair of oily gloves.

Smoke wafted out through the crevices in the car door's glass. Wasn't that Sanniu's brother? Sanniu's brother served as the driver for the commune secretary. Big Horse Face, capitalizing on Sanniu's brother's position, commandeered the small jeep to flaunt his status in Zhang Village.

At that moment, Xiuxiu's mother emerged from the house, holding Xiuxiu's younger sister in her arms, and began to cry. She sat down on the laundry stone in the yard. Big Horse Face then followed her out, with Xiuxiu trailing behind.

Big Horse Face wasn't smiling now; his face was even longer and more serious.

Xiuxiu's mother wept as she spoke, "Since the implementation of the household responsibility system, even district and county officials have managed to find time to return home and work on the farm. Yet you, on the contrary, never come home, and I haven't seen a single penny of your earnings. How dare you come here and request money from me!"

"Can you keep your voice down?" Big Horse Face said, stamping his foot.

"Who cares? Do you think others are oblivious to your affairs? Sooner or later... You tend to your business, and I'll tend to my stove; you relish your elaborate meals, and we'll savor our humble yam porridge... But bear in mind, if you neglect family matters, so will I. If you're seeking money, let me make it clear: there's none to be had!"

"What about the money you earned from your embroidery?" Big Horse Face asked.

"It's none of your business."

"I'm not asking for your money. It's really urgent right now. I promise I'll pay it back after a few days, how about that?"

"No way!" Xiuxiu's mother said, flicking her hair back.

"If you don't give me the money, I'll take Xiuxiu with me. Xiuxiu, let's go, there's a play at the commune!" Big Horse Face said with a stern face.

Xiuxiu was hiding behind a large locust tree, clutching it tightly with both arms, as if she was really afraid of being taken away.

"Come on!" Big Horse Face waved at Xiuxiu.

Xiuxiu clung even tighter to the tree, crying, "I won't go. I have to go to school!"

"School? Your school can't even afford a red tile. What kind of school is that? Dream on!" Big Horse Face's voice was louder this time, as if he was speaking to Auntie Xingfen.

Xiuxiu cried even more heartbrokenly.

Suddenly, Sanniu's brother swung open the car door and emerged. He removed his oil gloves and tossed them into the vehicle before proceeding to approach Xiuxiu. Despite her resistance, clinging to the tree, she refused to budge. Sanniu's brother attempted to coax her, saying, "Try sitting on the seat. Have you ever experienced the comfort of a soft chair? It's incredibly relaxing." As he spoke, he took Xiuxiu by surprise, grasping her armpits firmly with his large hands and hoisting her into the car.

Initially, Xiuxiu attempted to escape from the car, but Big Horse Face leaned into the window and pressed the circular wheel: "Beep beep!" The car emitted a sudden honk. Startled by the sound, Xiuxiu abandoned her efforts to escape. Instead, she mimicked Big Horse Face's action and pressed the wheel with her hand, causing the car to honk once more. Big Horse Face chuckled, then turned to Xiuxiu's mother with a smile, remarking, "Let's come to an agreement first. Don't come crying to me about your child in a few days. Think about it carefully!"

"There's nothing to consider. Xiuxiu, get down from the car!" Xiuxiu's mother, with child in her hands, hurried after them, speaking angrily.

Seeing that there was no hope, Big Horse Face slammed the car door on his side, and Sanniu's brother did the same on his side. The jeep emitted a puff of smoke and drove away. A flock of chickens, startled by the noise, flew up onto the rooftops.

Xiuxiu's mother stamped her foot and declared, "Even if you take the child away, I won't give you a single penny!"

After the jeep left, a smell of gasoline wafted over from the other side of the wall. Yuhu thought angrily: I was even considering letting you attend my aunt's school. How foolish I am! Go and ride your little jeep! Don't think you're the only one in the world who's good to me!

Who takes the empty seats?

The construction of the preschool is nearly finished, but it's still not usable. Why? Firstly, there are no windows installed on the walls, and secondly, there's no blackboard in the room. Why haven't these been taken care of? It's because Uncle Gao and the other workers have gone to the contracted fields to combat the drought.

This spring, the area was plagued by a severe drought. The corn ceased growing, stunted at just a few inches tall, its leaves wilting throughout the day. Newly planted millet and sorghum seedlings struggled to germinate. In such trying times, not only Uncle Gao but also Auntie Xingfen, had to join the battle against the drought. Even Yuhu couldn't remain idle at home, eagerly awaiting the start of school. The moment he witnessed his aunt heading out to combat the drought, he instinctively grabbed a washbasin and followed her all day, tirelessly scooping water from the river to the west of the village to irrigate the fields. After many days of dedicated effort, when Uncle Gao finally found some free time, he installed the windows and painted the blackboard.

With the windows and blackboards in

place, Yuhu finally felt like the old house had transformed into a school. Even though there was still no red roof, his aunt was the teacher of this school, so he had no reason to leave. Besides, he couldn't let Big Horse Face mock it. Now, he eagerly anticipated the day when his aunt would stand in front of the real blackboard and begin teaching.

That day finally arrived. Auntie Xingfen put on her clean clothes when she wore in high school in the town. She stood in front of the blackboard, opened a white paper notebook, and said, "Class!"

As soon as Xingfen called out "class," a giggle escaped from someone below. With one person leading the laughter, all the children in the room joined in. However, Xingfen didn't laugh, despite usually being the most easygoing. She placed her hands on the lectern and spoke solemnly, "Please refrain from laughing, because from today onward, you are the true students of our Zhang Village. Now, I will begin taking attendance. When I call your name, stand up and say 'here'. For instance, if I call Yu Meihua, Yu Meihua should stand up and say 'here', then sit down. Now, let's begin—Yu Meihua."

"Present!" The child named Meihua followed Auntie Xingfen's instructions correctly and stood up to respond.

"Wang Erxing!"

"Present!" Erxing also stood up and said correctly.

"Zhang Dabao!"

Zhang Dabao quickly said, "Ah!" But he didn't stand up.

As soon as Dabao responded with "Ah," the room burst into laughter once more.

Auntie Xingfen said, "Never mind, you'll get used to it gradually. If anyone laughs again, I'll invite that person to come to the front and sing a song for us. Who wants to sing?"

The students indeed quieted down. Then, Auntie Xingfen continued to call out names: Zhang Yuhu, Zhang Xiaorong, Yu Xiaojun, Wang Qinglin... She also called out Wang Sanniu, Li Xiaozhu, and Lin Xiuxiu. Auntie Xingfen called out the names of over forty people in one breath.

When Auntie Xingfen called out the names of Sanniu, Xiaozhu, and Xiuxiu, the students glanced around the classroom, half-expecting to find them seated somewhere. However, they were nowhere to be seen, only several vacant seats remained. Sanniu wouldn't be attending school at this time, and without Sanniu, Xiaozhu would also be absent. As for Lin Xiuxiu, she hadn't returned to Zhang Village since her father took her away in the jeep that day. Additionally, there were other students who were absent for various reasons. Now, Auntie Xingfen deliberately called out their names towards these empty seats to signify that they were still regarded as students of the preschool, and not to be treated as outsiders.

Although Yuhu was Xingfen's cousin, he was not ready for the roll call. He had no objections when others were called, but he couldn't agree with calling the names of those three individuals. Some students were eager to go to the street to find Sanniu and Xiaozhu, but Yuhu just remained silent with his head down. Auntie Xingfen, of course, understood Yuhu's feelings at a glance. She smiled and changed the topic.

In the evening, upon returning home, Yuhu remained upset with his aunt and declined to partake in dinner. He retrieved a piece of scrap paper from the drawer, deftly folding it into an aeroplane. With deliberate nonchalance, he tossed it towards the ceiling under the lamplight, feigning ignorance of his aunt's presence. On one occasion, it nearly landed in the rice pot, eliciting a disapproving glance from his grandparents, who pondered, "What's amiss with this child?"

Auntie Xingfen rolled her eyes and said, "I know, Yuhu thinks our school lacks a sufficient number of students."

"That's not," Yuhu pouted.

"Or do you think there are too many students?" Auntie Xingfen asked with a smile.

"Exactly, I think there are too many students!" Yuhu thought: If only you had known my thoughts earlier. People like Wang Sanniu, Li Xiaozhu, and even Lin Xiuxiu, they don't deserve to have their names called. And you, you not only call their names but also save seats for them.

"So, tell me, do you think it's better for our school to have more students or fewer?" Auntie Xingfen asked Yuhu again.

"Just right is good! Except those three, anyone else is welcome!"

"I understand why you don't welcome Sanniu to school. But what has Xiaozhu done to you?" Auntie Xingfen asked Yuhu.

"He does whatever Sanniu tells him to do!"

"What about Lin Xiuxiu?"

"Her father is Big Horse Face, and she's not from our village!"

It seemed that Auntie Xingfen couldn't

convince Yuhu for the time being. After a moment, she asked, "What if they come to school?"

"Just Drive them out!"

"Alright, I'll find them tomorrow and ask them to come to school; and you, just be ready to drive them out."

Yuhu stopped talking.

The following day, after breakfast, Xingfen indeed rallied all the students to embark on a quest to visit each household in search of the missing trio. Witnessing his classmates eagerly joining the effort, Yuhu reluctantly trailed behind. Their first encounter was with Qiaozhen in a narrow lane.

Ever since Qiaozhen confided in Xingfen about her father's intention to purchase her a knitting machine, her father, who served as a procurement officer in the town, indeed procured one for her. Qiaozhen was en route somewhere, carrying a bundle of wool yarn, when she spotted Xingfen approaching. She contemplated turning away, but Auntie Xingfen addressed her, refraining from mentioning the knitting machine. Instead, she said, "Qiaozhen, we've come to locate your brother and invite him to join us at school."

"Oh. If he comes back, I'll inform him," Qiaozhen said, imitating the accent from people outside the village.

Yuhu stood at a distance, thinking: After selling a few sweaters outside, she started to speak in a weird tone by using the pedantic "if" and "inform". Who doesn't know you're from Zhang Village?

"I didn't expect you to really start the school. I haven't had a chance to congratulate you yet," Qiaozhen said, trying to start a conversation.

"It's a collective effort, supported by the Party branch," Xingfen said. "When you have time, visit and give us your suggestions."

Qiaozhen thought for a moment and said, "Ah, look at how busy I am." With that, she left, still holding her wool yarn.

Xingfen watched her leave and said, "When Sanniu comes back, try to persuade him to come!"

"Sure. This child really needs some discipline," Qiaozhen agreed, turning her head.

Xingfen emerged from the alley and approached the home of a child named Zhang Xiaorong. Xiaorong's mother quickly appeared to greet her. She was relatively young and still wore her hair in two plaits. Upon seeing Xingfen, she immediately understood that the visit was related to Xiaorong's schooling. Hastily, she retrieved a schoolbag from the house and presented it to Auntie Xingfen, explaining, "Look, we've already bought the schoolbag, but she's afraid of going to school. This child is quite timid; she hasn't dared to attend nursery for a long time now."

"Oh," Auntie Xingfen smiled, "This time, there's nothing to worry about. We have many people. I'll come to pick her up tomorrow. Where is Xiaorong?"

"Who knows where she went in a blink of eyes," Xiaorong's mother replied.

As soon as Xiaorong's mother finished speaking, a little girl's head poked out from the room. She was very thin and weak, with big eyes that blinked as if she is saying, "I'm right here."

Auntie Xingfen quickly spotted Xiaorong

and grasped the situation. Taking Xiaorong by the hand, Xingfen guided her outside, helped her put on the new backpack, and remarked, "You look just like a student now. Let's go and find your seat." With that, she led Xiaorong and the other students out of the courtyard.

They then went to the home of a child named Wang Qinglin. Wang Qinglin was sitting on the steps, babysitting his younger sister.

"Where are your parents?" Xingfen asked.

"They went to plough the fields," Wang Qinglin replied.

As they conversed, Wang Qinglin's mother entered with a plough. Upon seeing Xingfen, she leaned the plough against the wall and remarked, "Ever since the household responsibility system came into effect, we haven't been able to afford a cow yet. Qinglin keeps pleading to go to school. We'll allow him once we're done ploughing and have someone available to care for his sister."

They finally arrived at Xiaozhu's house. Xiaozhu wasn't home, and his mother said, "Xingfen, this child, he drives us crazy every day, and now he's causing you so much trouble!"

Xingfen smiled and said, "We can't just blame Xiaozhu. It's not all his fault. I'll come back tomorrow to find him. Or I will let Yuhu come. Yuhu has been wanting to play with Xiaozhu for a while now."

"That would be great," Xiaozhu's mother said, noticing Yuhu standing behind them and speaking loudly, "I was worried that Yuhu doesn't want to hang out with him. If this child could just follow Yuhu, that would be so much better!"

Upon hearing Auntie Xingfen's words and Xiaozhu's mother's praise, Yuhu was struck by a twinge of guilt regarding Xiaozhu. After all, there were several occasions when Xiaozhu had attempted to play with him, but Yuhu had intentionally avoided him. He couldn't help but wonder if his kindness towards Xiaozhu could have prevented Xiaozhu from following Sanniu instead.

"At least, I have a good mum!"

Under Auntie Xingfen's guidance, the number of students in the preschool class did indeed grow, with nearly every seat filled. After a couple of days, Xiaozhu, who had been hesitant, also expressed a desire to enter the school gate. Yuhu took the initiative to guide him into the classroom, not only assisting him in entering but also personally showing him to his seat.

Only Sanniu was absent. Since the preschool opened, the number of his followers had dwindled day by day. Now, with Xiaozhu starting school, his group had shrunk to just two or three children still in open-crotch pants. As the fun had diminished, Sanniu disbanded them. As for himself, sometimes he would squat on the wall of the preschool, tossing clods of dirt into the classroom; other times, he would lurk behind corners or trees near the school gate to startle the students. However, the students always left the school in an orderly line, marching straight ahead without acknowledging him. Grandma Wubao beamed with joy as she stood on the street, unable to contain her happiness. Turning to

Auntie Xingfen, she exclaimed, "This is what you meant by standing up for me!"

In the classroom, two seats remained vacant. One, unquestionably, belonged to Sanniu as it was placed at the end to accommodate his height. The other seat, situated in front of Yuhu's, was reserved for Xiuxiu. Yuhu was aware of this and deliberately avoided looking at the seat, knowing it was reserved for Xiuxiu by his aunt.

Where has Xiuxiu been lately? She's been residing with her father at the commune's brick and tile factory. She deeply regrets the day she mimicked her father by honking the horn of the little jeep. If not for that action, she would have never ended up at this location in the jeep.

Xiuxiu had only heard about the brick

and tile factory before, never seeing it until now. Now, she understood: the factory boasted a vast courtyard and a sizable iron gate. Within the yard stood brick kilns that loomed like miniature mountains, stacks of red and grey bricks forming walls, and several rows of houses. Her father resided in the first one. Each day, her father would venture to the supply and marketing cooperative to procure snacks and fried dough sticks for her. Xiuxiu wondered where her father acquired such funds. She knew it was from winning at gambling. Every evening, their room transformed into a gambling den where people would play "Gou Niu" on a small table within the kang, covering the windows with blankets. The games would stretch into the early hours of the morning, accompanied by drinking and feasting, creating such a racket that Xiuxiu struggled to sleep through the night.

Does Xiuxiu not long to return to Zhang Village? Of course, she does. Despite having rice and white flour every day, Xiuxiu yearns for the yam porridge from her grandmother's house in Zhang Village, and she misses her mother. Her mother taught her the value of living frugally, while her father indulges in feasts here, even asking her mother for money—how unreasonable! Xiuxiu not only misses her grandmother and mother but also misses Yuhu next door. Yuhu and the others must have gone to school with backpacks that have zippers. If Xiuxiu knew that Aunt Xingfen had saved a seat for her, she would risk everything to run back to Zhang Village.

Xiuxiu made several attempts to return and find her mother, but Big Horse Face wouldn't allow it. No matter how heartbroken she cried, Big Horse Face ignored her, even accusing her of ingratitude. At times, Xiuxiu felt an urge to walk back on her own. However, the commune was more than ten miles away from Zhang Village, and she didn't know the way. Each day passed with Xiuxiu waiting and longing for the chance to go back.

One day, while peering through the window, Xiuxiu overheard two people in the courtyard discussing the factory's truck going to Zhang Village to collect grain. Her heart raced with excitement. She thought, "Yuhu and Xiaozhu once came to town on a cart loaded with cotton, didn't they? Why can't I ride the grain truck back to my grandmother's house?" She climbed onto her bed, leaned against the windowsill, and gazed out into the yard. To her delight, there was a large truck parked right outside her window. Without hesitation, she opened the window and, with a swing of her legs, stepped onto the truck.

Fortunately, there was a stack of empty burlap sacks in the truck. Xiuxiu quickly grabbed one and draped it over herself, then lay down on the pile of sacks. The two people who had been talking had both moved into the driver's cab, and neither of them noticed her.

The truck honked loudly, causing Xiuxiu to jolt within the sacks as the vehicle started its journey. She rolled and swayed with the sacks throughout the trip. As the sun began to set, they were well on their way, and by dusk, they had reached Zhang Village.

Every morning, the first thing Yuhu did upon opening his eyes was to go to the yard and release the chickens from their coop. On this particular day, after setting the chickens free and watching the big rooster and the clucking hen fly up onto the wall, he was about to turn around and head back to wash his face. However, he couldn't help but notice what seemed like a little dog's tail flitting from the other side of the wall. Yuhu scolded himself silently, "Why am I thinking of her again? Nonsense!" He refrained from turning his head to look over the wall, instead pretending to call the chickens down to eat. Just then, as Yuhu called out to the chickens, someone indeed called his name from atop the wall, "Yuhu!"

Upon hearing the voice, Yuhu recognized it as sounding like Xiuxiu's. "Whoever you are!" Yuhu, still facing away, grabbed a handful of grain from the basket by the wall and tossed it to the chickens. Just then, the voice calling his name, "Yuhu!" came again from the other side of the wall.

Yuhu thought, could it really be Xiuxiu coming back? If it is, so be it. But he resolved not to look over there no matter what. He wanted to go inside to wash his face, but then the voice from the wall shouted again, "It's me, Xiuxiu!"

Yuhu stopped, with his back to the wall, and called out, "I know who you are. Why are you calling me?"

"Look at my schoolbag. It also has zipper."

It turned out that while Xiuxiu was away, her mother spent each day eagerly anticipating her return. Upon learning from Xingfen that the school had reserved a seat for Xiuxiu, her mother's longing intensified. She resolved to gift Xiuxiu a new schoolbag and arranged for someone from the county supply and marketing cooperative to purchase it, requesting that it have a zipper.

Now, as soon as Xiuxiu mentioned the schoolbag with zippers, Yuhu thought to himself, "Wasn't it me who told you about it?" Without turning around, he went into the house.

It turned out that while Xiuxiu was away, her mother spent each day eagerly anticipating her return. Upon learning from Xingfen that the school had reserved a seat for Xiuxiu, her mother's longing intensified. She resolved to gift Xiuxiu a new schoolbag and arranged for someone from the county supply and marketing cooperative to purchase it, requesting that it have a zipper.

She led her to the front of the classroom and announced to everyone, "Class, I've brought a new student here. Look who is she. Aren't you going to clap and welcome her?"

"It's Xiuxiu!"

"Lin Xiuxiu!"

The students started to buzz with excitement, and some even clapped their hands. Yuhu glanced sideways with a grumble, "What's the point of clapping?"

Xingfen continued, "Actually, Lin Xiuxiu is already an old classmate of us. Look at her seat, hasn't it been empty all this time? Xiuxiu, go and take your seat."

Xingfen pointed to the empty seat for Xiuxiu, who then sat down with her school bag.

"Alright, let's begin the lesson now. Today we're learning arithmetic. Everyone, please look at the blackboard and copy the numbers into your notebooks. When you've finished, I'll give you grades." As Xingfen spoke, she picked up the chalk and quickly wrote down the numbers from 10 to 15 on the blackboard.

As Xiuxiu sat down in front of Yuhu, he began to feel a bit uncomfortable. Trying to copy the numbers from the blackboard, he found it even more inconvenient than before. The head with the little dog-tail plait in front of him constantly blocked half of the blackboard. Additionally, since Xiuxiu had just arrived, she struggled with writing correctly. Her lack of proficiency led her to tilt her head more, which only irritated Yuhu further. He resolved to find his aunt and request a change of seat as soon as the class ended.

Interestingly, Yuhu could write from 1 to 100 without needing to look at the blackboard. However, for some reason, he found that the little dog-tail plait in front of him was causing a slight hindrance in his learning. Consequently, it wasn't until the end of the class that he managed to write five numbers, his brow furrowed in concentration. Suddenly, and for reasons unknown to him, he leaned sideways and discreetly glanced at the desk in front of him. On the desk lay Xiuxiu's notebook, relatively new, yet the numbers inscribed within resembled overgrown bean sprouts.

As his aunt approached, Xiuxiu remained calm. Believing she had performed well, she raised her notebook to hand it in. However, Yuhu couldn't hold back any longer. Ignoring past grievances, he leaned over to gently tap Xiuxiu's back and whispered, "Hey, you can't turn it in yet!"

Just as Xiuxiu was about to turn around to speak, Auntie Xingfen walked over, smiled at her, and took the notebook away.

School ended, and Yuhu, without waiting

for the dismissal line, dashed out of the school gate. He sighed, reproaching himself for the events of the day. If only he had acted like a seasoned student in the morning when Xiuxiu called out to him, explaining to her what they had learned in the arithmetic lesson, perhaps he wouldn't have found himself in this situation.

He ran all the way home and stood by the chicken coop, waiting for Xiuxiu's return. As soon as Xiuxiu entered the door, before she even had a chance to look towards the wall, Yuhu called out to her.

"Lin Xiuxiu!" Yuhu called out to her, addressing her in the way of calling a classmate.

Xiuxiu turned her head and, upon seeing Yuhu, felt a bit shy and hesitated to walk forward.

"Come over here already!" Yuhu whispered, urging her on.

Xiuxiu, holding her schoolbag strap, walked over.

"What kind of numbers have you written? It looks like a mess of rotten bean sprouts!" Yuhu stared straight at Xiuxiu as he spoke.

"I don't know that," Xiuxiu replied. Her own handwriting looked as displeasing to her as it did to Yuhu.

"Why didn't you ask me?"

"You even turned away when I asked you to take care of my new school bag. How could I dare to ask you about my homework?"

"It is you riding in a jeep!"

When Yuhu mentioned the jeep, Xiuxiu was momentarily speechless once more. She lowered her head, reflecting for a moment before admitting, "It was my fault for riding in the jeep, but I blame that horn—it honked with just a press!"

"Hmph, you rode in it, so what? Blaming the horn for it," Yuhu still didn't understand.

"But I came back on my own!"

"I don't believe! The commune is so far away. How can you run back?"

"Isn't the town far too? Yet you've been there!"

"We have a big cart!"

"I rode on a bus."

"It's you father's jeep."

"That's not. It was a big truck. I hid inside the burlap sacks, and when the truck jolted, it was really terrifying," Xiuxiu said, her voice full of excitement.

"I still don't believe," Yuhu said, even though he was already feeling sorry for Xiuxiu.

"If you don't believe me, you can ask my

mum!"

" You are families. She will speak up for you."

"No, she won't!" Xiuxiu thought Yuhu was referring to her father and mother. "My mum says, 'You enjoy your fine meals, and I will have porridge with my children.' Listen, is my mum speak up for my dad?"

"Anyway, your dad is not a good person," Yuhu bluntly shifted the conversation back to Xiuxiu's father.

With tears in her eyes, Xiuxiu said, "My dad may not be good, but at least I still have a good mum!"

The aeroplane that can make it rain

After establishing the school for the

children, the young people of Zhang Village returned to the fields to tackle the drought. Each person had their designated field, and they worked diligently. However, families with a shortage of labor were feeling anxious.

Grandpa Wugeng was known for his regular visits from house to house, assisting those facing difficulties. Observing his anxiety, Xingfen initiated a conversation, saying, "Our school's students will also participate in the drought relief efforts, assisting families lacking labor. Just assign us the tasks." Upon returning to the school, Xingfen made arrangements, and soon children brought basins and ladles from home. Under Yuhu's guidance, the kindergarten's drought relief team swiftly assembled at the western part of the village. Not long ago, everyone had elected Yuhu as the class monitor. From a distance,

Grandpa Wugeng exclaimed, "Look, this is the children's scout of the drought relief army."

The children scouts worked with tremendous enthusiasm, forming groups of three or two and using basins to scoop water from the river. Whenever they arrived at someone's home, the adults there would be delighted, smiling broadly. However, perhaps due to the excessively dry ground or the children's young age, despite their strenuous efforts, they could only manage to water a small patch of land after a considerable amount of time.

During the break, Xiaozhu ran over to Xingfen and asked, "Miss Zhang, Sanniu said there are aeroplanes that can make it rain. Is that true? Why don't they fly over here?"

Upon hearing that it was Sanniu, Yuhu thought that Xiaozhu was deliberately trying to make things difficult for Xingfen. He quickly retorted, "Why can't you just forget what Sanniu said!"

To his surprise, aunt Xingfen replied, "There are aeroplanes that can make it rain. If you're interested, we can talk about it in class tomorrow."

Knowing that Yuhu knew how to fold paper aeroplanes, Xingfen asked him to teach her how to do it during dinner. The next day, she brought the paper aeroplane to class.

She stood in front of the podium, took out the aeroplane from her bag, and held it up, saying, "Class, look what's this?"

"An aeroplane!" everyone answered in unison.

"Correct, it's an aeroplane. Yesterday someone told me that he wanted to learn about aeroplanes that can rain, so today we'll talk about it. However, to understand how aeroplanes can produce raindrops, you need to know many things first. For instance, who can explain to us how does rain form?"

Xiaozhu stood up without hesitation and said, "I know. My mum says there's an old man in the sky who pours water from his washbasin, and every time he pours, it rains."

"That's not right!" it was Xiaorong who corrected Xiaozhu. "My grandma says there's a housewife in the sky, and when she cries, it rains."

"Do you guys agree?" Xingfen asked the class.

For a moment, the classroom was silent. Some students, although they knew that what the two had said was incorrect, didn't know how to provide the right answer either.

Xingfen smiled and responded, "Actually,

both of those are incorrect. There are alternative stories that suggest there's a god of thunder in the sky, depicted as a man with a sharp tongue and two horns, driving a cart filled with water. On this cart, there's a drum, and whenever he strikes it, thunder is produced, and when he pours water, it rains. The god of thunder is also said to have a wife known as the goddess of lightning. She wields two mirrors, and by shaking them vigorously, lightning is generated. However, these are all superstitions from the feudal society."

"So, how does it actually rain?" Xiaorong asked, eager for the correct explanation.

"Let me explain," Xingfen began. "In simple terms, rain comes from water vapor. You know when you lift the lid off a pot while cooking at home, and you see many water droplets on it? It's similar to how water vapor transforms into rain. Our planet has a lot of water—rivers, lakes, puddles, and the ocean. When the sun shines on the water, a lot of heat rises into the sky. As it ascends, it forms clouds." As Xingfen spoke, she used chalk to draw on the blackboard, illustrating how the white vapor turned into clouds. "Now, when these clouds encounter cold air in the sky, what do you think will happen? Take a moment to think about it."

Several children raised their hands at the same time. Xingfen pointed to Xiaozhu and said, "Xiaozhu, please share your ideas?"

"It..."

"It turns into water!" Yuhu answered urgently.

"What happens when the water falls from the sky? This time, let Xiaozhu answer," Xingfen said, waving her hand at Yuhu to indicate that he should sit down.

"It's rain," Xiaozhu finally got the right answer.

"Exactly, that's rain," Xingfen said, and then she drew many white lines beneath the clouds.

"Why isn't it raining now? Aren't there clouds in the sky?" Xiuxiu asked the teacher, pointing at the window.

"It's up to you," Xingfen said.

"To us?" the class asked simultaneously.

"Yes, it depends on you," Xingfen affirmed confidently. "Sometimes, even if there are many clouds, the atmosphere isn't cold enough in the sky, so it won't rain. That's where you come in. You need to take a special kind of medicine, board an aeroplane, and ascend into the sky. Once you're up there, you scatter the medicine, cooling the clouds. When the clouds cool down sufficiently, rain will begin to pour."

"Can we go to the sky?"

"Of course you can!" Xingfen said with more certainty, "But first, you have to learn these skills—building aeroplanes, piloting them, making the medicine, and sprinkling it. To learn these skills, you need education. Then, when I call out names, whoever I point to can pilot the aeroplane. Students, think about it, what would it be like to control the rain from the sky in an aeroplane?"

At night, Yuhu had a dream: He came to school with his schoolbag and saw an aeroplane parked in the schoolyard, waiting for him to fly it. He climbed into the cockpit.

As soon as Yuhu settled, Xiaozhu came running towards the aeroplane carrying a washbasin. Yuhu asked him from inside,

"What are you doing with a washbasin?"

"I'm carrying the medicine to scatter it down!"

At that moment, Xiuxiu also came running over with a sprayer on her shoulder. As she ran, she said to Xiaozhu, "I've got a sprayer. This is better!"

Finally, Aunt Xingfen also stepped into the aeroplane. As soon as she got on, she said to Yuhu, "Take off!"

Yuhu, feeling a bit nervous, pulled the control stick, and sure enough, the aeroplane lifted off from the school's yard.

The aeroplane flew over Zhang Village, circling around it first. The villagers working in the fields to combat the drought quickly spotted the aircraft and began jumping and waving hello from below. Grandpa Wugeng waved back at them and shouted, "Start by heading to our experimental fields. Let's ensure a good harvest there!"

Yuhu answered from the aeroplane, "Grandpa Wugeng, got it!"

Just then, a voice from below called out. It was Xiaozhu's mother. She shouted in a loud voice, "Zhu, wear more clothes. Be careful. Do not catch a cold!"

Upon hearing this, Yuhu said to Xiaozhu, "Your mum is the most talkative."

As the aeroplane continued its ascent, the people of Zhang Village gradually became smaller and smaller, their houses resembling matchboxes from such a height. Suddenly, the aircraft entered a vast cloud, obscuring everything from view. Yuhu turned to Xingfen and inquired, "Auntie, I can't see anything. Which way should I fly?"

"Keep going up. Fly through the clouds,"

aunt said.

After Yuhu pressed some buttons, the aeroplane surged upward and broke through the cloud layer. Now, all the clouds were beneath them, and above was the sunlit sky.

At that moment, Aunt Xingfen stood up in the aeroplane and ordered, "Now, it's time to disperse the medicine."

Xiaozhu held up the washbasin and said, "I'll do it now!" With that, he started to grab handfuls and scatter them.

Xiuxiu quickly said, "It's my turn!" She raised the sprayer and started spraying.

Xingfen directed, "Leap out of the aircraft and spray." With that command, she took the lead and leaped out of the cabin. However, the children remained somewhat hesitant. Yuhu displayed the most courage; he was the first to follow suit and jump out. Upon seeing Yuhu jump, Xiaozhu and Xiuxiu also summoned their bravery and leapt out of the plane.

Once the children had jumped out of the cabin, they attempted to walk on the clouds. Strangely, their steps were incredibly light, causing them to sway from side to side. It wasn't until the three of them stood shoulder to shoulder that they felt considerably more stable.

But when they looked at Aunt Xingfen, they saw she had already run quite far ahead. They quickened their pace, imitating Aunt Xingfen, scattering the medicine in all directions.

After scattering for a while, Xiaozhu looked up at the sky and asked Aunt Xingfen, "Why isn't it raining yet?"

Xingfen said from distance, "Look down below."

The three of them thought for a moment before realizing that they shouldn't look up, but to look down.

Yuhu parted a piece of cloud with his hand and peered down. To his astonishment, a downpour was already soaking the earth below. With the sun shining brightly from above, the raindrops appeared like colourful threads, stretching from the sky all the way to the ground.

As they looked on, they suddenly spotted a village. Yuhu excitedly called out, "Look, isn't that our Zhang Village?"

"How do you know?" Xiuxiu asked, stretching her neck to look down.

"Isn't that Sanniu?"

Upon hearing that Sanniu was down there, Xiaozhu immediately shouted loudly, "Hey— Sanniu!"

Sanniu, looking up from below, also called out, "Xiaozhu, give our Zhang Village more rain, our village is suffering from drought!"

As soon as Sanniu requested more rain from Xiaozhu, Xiaozhu swiftly grabbed the sprayer from Xiuxiu's hand and resumed spraying. However, as Xiaozhu began to spray, Grandpa Wugeng's voice boomed from below, "Who's doing that? Why won't it stop? We're getting flooded down here!" He then shouted, "Comrades, let's control the flood!"

As soon as the Grandpa shouted to fight the flood, Yuhu woke up.

The next day in class, Yuhu told Xiaozhu about his dream of flying an aeroplane up to the sky to scatter medicine and make it rain.

"It's all Sanniu's fault!" Yuhu said.

"Right, Sanniu should be blamed!" Xiaozhu agreed.

Hearing them mention Sanniu from the podium, Xingfen walked over and asked, "Yuhu, what's wrong with Sanniu?"

Yuhu thought for a moment, unsure of how to answer. As he looked around, he unexpectedly spotted Sanniu. It turned out that Sanniu was peering in through the window.

Yuhu pointed out the window and said, "There he is, right there!"

Xingfen put down the eraser and walked to the door, saying, "Sanniu, are you here to attend school?"

Sanniu didn't talk.

"Is your sister sent you there?" Xingfen asked again.

"No," Sanniu replied.

"Are you willing to come here?"

"Yes."

"That's even better. Come on in, look, there's still a seat for you," Xingfen stepped aside, welcoming Sanniu to enter.

Just as Sanniu was about to enter with a grin, someone in the classroom shouted loudly, "Miss Zhang, he has cigarettes in his pocket!"

Another classmate said, "He also has a knife tucked in his waist!"

Some students shouted out other things as well.

These words clearly made an impression on Sanniu. He widened his eyes in surprise and challenged the class, "You're just crying 'stop thief'! If you don't believe me, search me!" With that, he turned his pockets inside out, displaying them to the class.

Xingfen approached, fixing Sanniu's pockets and remarking, "It's good you don't carry those items. We can't keep behaving like this." She mimicked a fighting stance similar to Sanniu's. "Now, button up your shirt. Your hat is crooked." After adjusting Sanniu's hat, she guided him into the classroom.

Key moment

As soon as school resumed, Yuhu always found that time flew by incredibly quickly. In the blink of an eye, the millet had sprouted ears, the corn had grown as tall as a house, and it was time to prepare for the college entrance exams once more.

Yuhu's grandpa was looking forward to this day.

In previous years, the focus was on recommending students for university admission, and Grandpa always wore a stern expression. When Auntie expressed her desire to attend junior high school, Grandpa remarked, "What's the use of pursuing higher education? We lack connections and influence. Do you truly believe you can leave Zhang Village?" It wasn't until the implementation of the college entrance examination (Gaokao) that Grandpa would smile and say to Auntie, "We have a true high school graduate, someone with a solid education. A genuine high school graduate should aspire for greater heights."

Last year, knowing that Aunt Xingfen was only 3 points short, Grandpa said, "Next year, we'll surpass it by thirty points."

Upon Auntie's decision to start a school in the village, Grandpa's expression turned stern once more, indicating his disapproval. He likened Auntie's choice to that of a phoenix opting to remain in a chicken coop, suggesting he viewed it as a misfit or a step down from her potential.

One day, Xingfen returned from school, rolling up her sleeves to knead dough and steam buns, while Yuhu squatted in front of the stove, assisting his grandmother by operating the bellows. At that moment, Grandpa hummed a tune as he entered the yard with his hands behind his back. He stood in the middle of the yard, coughed once, but didn't proceed inside. Yuhu speculated that Grandpa must have some good news, prompting him to drop the firewood and head to the yard to join Grandpa.

Aunt was well aware of Grandpa's temperament. The more she understood him, the less she spoke, deliberately keeping her head down while cooking. Eventually, Grandpa couldn't contain himself any longer. With a smile, he called out to Yuhu, "Yuhu, come here!" even though Yuhu was standing right beside him. Grandpa then quickly retrieved a newspaper from behind his back and instructed, "Here! Take this to your aunt!"

Yuhu picked up the newspaper, unfolded it, and attempted to read. Unfortunately, his education was limited, and he struggled to recognize many characters. He closed the newspaper and decided to give it to Auntie. However, she deliberately didn't accept it, as if she already knew its contents. Instead, she smiled at Grandpa and said, "Dad, could you please read it for me?"

"I'll read it. Who says I can't read these characters!" Grandpa said, snatching the newspaper from Yuhu. He began to read,

"...University admission...admission..." but then he couldn't continue.

"Prospectus!" Auntie finished the sentence.

At that moment, Grandma smiled at Grandpa and said, "You old fool, look at you, so proud!"

"Xingfen, now that the time has come. What's your plan?" Grandpa ignored Grandma and asked Auntie directly.

"We have neither connections nor influence," Auntie replied, "You didn't ask what's the situation of university admissions this year?"

"Don't dig up my old stories. That was during the period of Gang of Four," Grandpa said. "Nowadays, the newspapers clearly state every year's enrollment is based on individual abilities and voluntary registration. It doesn't allow substitution and suppression. You are a genuine high school graduate."

"Ah!" Auntie feigned a sigh and said, "What's the point of getting higher education? Even though I get higher degree, it won't let me leave Zhang Village."

Yuhu knew that Aunt was deliberately using Grandpa's past words to get a rise out of him. But Yuhu was still unclear about Aunt's true intention.

A few days later, much like the previous year, the young people in the village began to immerse themselves in studying and gathering materials for review. Grandpa Wugeng even had several large slogans posted around the village, proclaiming, "This time, Zhang Village must produce some promising talents!"

It wasn't until Uncle Gao, Sister Caiyun, Auntie Xiaoxia, and Brother Chunlai were constantly carrying books to review with

Xingfen that Yuhu knew what Auntie was thinking.

It appeared that Auntie remained resolute in preparing for the college entrance exam. Throughout the day, she taught lessons at school, and at night, upon returning home to her small room in the west of the yard, her light would remain on until midnight. Visitors who came to study with Xingfen would sit on the heated brick bed (kang). Xingfen even hung a small blackboard on the wall. Whenever someone posed a question, she would write and solve it on the blackboard.

In recent days, the students at the preschool had also been talking about this matter. Whenever they had the chance, they would gather around Yuhu and ask him about it.

"Of course, she's going to the exam!" Yuhu

imitated his grandpa's tone and said to them, "My aunt is a genuine high school graduate!"

Yuhu expressed happiness when he made that statement, but afterward, he inexplicably felt a wave of sadness. Could it be that he didn't want his aunt to become a university student? Certainly not. Ultimately, he was afraid that if his aunt left, their school would be shut down.

The sentiments of the other students mirrored Yuhu's. Take Sanniu, for instance. He had been performing exceptionally well lately, being tall, quick to learn characters, and consistently receiving praise. Upon hearing about Xingfen's plans to take the college entrance exam, he also became curious to verify its truth. One night, Sanniu gathered his old "Gorilla" team, and they stealthily entered Xingfen's yard. As expected, the light was on in her small room. Sanniu quietly moved along the wall towards the window, stood on tiptoes, and peered through the glass into the room. Inside, Xingfen was standing in front of the small blackboard, explaining questions to everyone. The equations she was writing were much longer than those taught in class, and some even included foreign characters.

After getting a clear look, Sanniu crouched down, waved his hand at the other children behind him, and then quietly slipped out of the yard. Once they were out, Sanniu shared the information he had personally gathered with them. It appeared certain that their teacher was indeed planning to leave.

The next day, during the arithmetic class, after taking attendance, Xingfen addressed the students, saying, "Today, we're going to work on arithmetic. I'll give you all a math problem." Pausing briefly to think, she continued, "Yesterday, Xiaozhu's mother and Xiaorong's mother both went to the field to hoe the corn. Xiaozhu's mother hoed five rows in the first half of the day, and Xiaorong's mother hoed four rows. How many rows did they hoe together?"

After saying this, Xingfen wrote a simple addition problem on the blackboard: 5 + 4.

Xiaozhu immediately raised his hand. Noticing the serious expression on Xiaozhu's face, Xingfen said, "Xiaozhu, you please."

Unexpectedly, as soon as Xiaozhu stood up, he said, "Miss Zhang, my mum didn't hoe the corn yesterday; she went to Dazhang Village to sell eggs at the market."

Upon hearing this, Xingfen couldn't help but burst into laughter. As soon as Xingfen laughed, everyone in the room joined in and laughed as well.

But Xiaozhu remained serious as he stood there. Xingfen managed to hold back her laughter and asked again, "Zhu, let me ask you this: it's six li to get to Da Zhangzhuang for the market, and another six li to come back. What's the total distance?" After saying this, she wrote another addition problem on the blackboard: 6 + 6.

Xiaozhu thought for a moment and tried to count on his fingers, but he ran out of fingers. Embarrassed, he lowered his head.

Xingfen said, "Zhu, you may sit down. Who can answer this question?"

Several classmates raised their hands together. Those who didn't raise their hands were also thinking seriously.

"Put your hands down please," Xingfen said.

The children all put their hands down. At that moment, Sanniu suddenly raised his hand and said, "Miss Zhang, look, Li Xiaozhu is still counting on his fingers. How silly!"

Sanniu was sitting behind Xiaozhu. After speaking, he stretched out his foot and kicked Xiaozhu's seat, saying, "Sit down. What are you waiting for?"

Unexpectedly, Xingfen's tone turned serious all of a sudden. She remarked, "While Sanniu has shown considerable progress recently, one should not become arrogant merely due to praise. Your attitude towards Xiaozhu just now was not commendable, and your speech was impolite. Among classmates, our role is to support each other, not to mock or belittle anyone. We must maintain politeness and refrain from insulting others. Moreover, how can you be certain that

Xiaozhu cannot solve the problem?" After speaking, Xingfen cast a concerned look towards Xiaozhu.

Xiaozhu fixed a challenging gaze upon Sanniu and murmured softly, "Merely because you're adept at calculations doesn't imply I'm not. Be it three sixes, four sixes, or a myriad of sixes, the tutor can guide me through. You'll see!"

Xingfen listened to Xiaozhu's words and nodded in agreement, saying, "Xiaozhu is correct. No matter how complex the problem is, I can teach you. If it requires a day, then two days; if two days are insufficient, then three days. Even if it takes a hundred days or a thousand, I will continue teaching you."

Once school had ended and the last of the students had departed through the school gates, Sanniu and a few other children encircled Xiaozhu. With a stern look, Sanniu exclaimed, "Li Xiaozhu, there's no one quite like you! Miss Zhang is on the verge of leaving, and yet you persist in clinging to her, requesting lessons on a thousand sixes, ten thousand sixes. How utterly shameless!"

At that moment, Yuhu also came over. Sanniu said, "Don't believe me? Ask Yuhu!"

When Sanniu suggested that Xiaozhu ask Yuhu, Yuhu remained silent and did not respond. This silence from Yuhu made Xiaozhu feel increasingly remorseful as if he had made a significant mistake. "I didn't know," Xiaozhu said, sounding bewildered.

"Yuhu," Sanniu said, "Go home and tell your aunt not to focus on the fake girl and delay her own matters!"

Yuhu quietly said "Okay", and then headed home.

As Xiaozhu was about to leave, Sanniu called out to him.

"Fake girl, come with us tomorrow. We're going to the town."

"You're not going to school?" Xiaozhu asked in surprise.

"There's something more important than going to school!"

Between friends

Normally, once the students had settled into the classroom, Xingfen would arrive promptly with her books tucked under her arm. However, this particular afternoon, despite everyone having been seated for quite some time, there was still no sign of Xingfen. Yuhu remembered that just before leaving home, he had seen Grandpa Wugeng seeking out his aunt, presumably to discuss matters regarding university enrolment.

In the absence of a teacher, the classroom grew a bit noisy. Some students stood up to peer out into the yard, while others engaged in light-hearted pushing and joking. Dabao and Erxing even began chasing each other around the tables. Then, a boy leaped onto a desk from the back and exclaimed, "Hey, everyone, hold on! I've got a magic trick to show you!" As all heads turned in his direction, they realized it was Sanniu.

Sanniu had fashioned a paper tube into a triangular shape, drawing the face of an elderly gentleman on it to create the illusion of an old man wearing a tall hat. Balancing it on his thumb, he deftly maneuvered it before everyone's eyes, at times concealing it under his armpit and at others behind his neck, all the while murmuring, "Today the old man is in, tomorrow the old man is out, the day after tomorrow the old man is in again!" The "old man's face" on his thumb would appear and vanish with his perplexing movements.

Sanniu's performance was so captivating that even Yuhu was a bit mesmerized.

Surprisingly, Xiaozhu, usually a quiet student in class, exhibited an unusual behavior. He had fashioned a paper tube and was mimicking Sanniu's performance flawlessly, reciting with a sense of pride, "Today the old man is at home, tomorrow the old man is not at home..." The "old man's face" on his thumb also appeared and disappeared in perfect sync with his gestures.

The classmates began to cheer, yet Sanniu couldn't shake off a tinge of disappointment.

He believed this was Xiaozhu's way of getting back at him for the arithmetic dispute earlier that day. Interrupting loudly, he declared, "This is dull! Let's cease this. Since Miss Zhang is departing, let's select a different teacher!"

"How do you know Miss Zhang is leaving?" someone asked.

"I saw it. Miss Zhang was reviewing, and there were foreign characters written on the blackboard," Sanniu replied.

Ordinarily, no one would typically take Sanniu's words seriously. However, when Sanniu mentioned that Miss Zhang was indeed reviewing, everyone in the classroom believed him. The room fell silent, and Sanniu, perched on the desk, turned to Yuhu and asked, "Yuhu, do you agree to select a new teacher?"

Yuhu initially considered voicing his disagreement, but then he pondered the situation. With his aunt departing and Grandpa Wugeng not having designated a replacement teacher yet, it seemed reasonable to opt for a new instructor. Otherwise, there might be remarks like, "Is your aunt the sole teacher? Can't someone else take over?" Thus, Yuhu consented, "Let's choose another one."

As soon as Yuhu agreed, the classroom buzzed with noise again. One student said, "I'll be the teacher." Another chimed in, "I will!"

"Suggest Yuhu as the teacher!" Sanniu proposed. He reasoned that despite Yuhu not speaking with him for several days, Yuhu was more educated than the others. Moreover, Yuhu had a close relationship with his Aunt Xingfen.

Several hands went up in agreement. Yuhu

was about to voice his opinion when a small voice from the front cut in, "No, that won't do. Yuhu isn't a girl, but Miss Zhang is." It was Xiaorong who made this observation.

"Then you be the teacher!" Sanniu said bluntly.

"I can't. But Xiuxiu can be!" Xiao Rong said, already having her nominee.

"Xiuxiu for teacher! Xiuxiu for teacher!" The classmates suddenly started to support Xiuxiu.

Xiuxiu glanced around and then at Yuhu. Seeing Yuhu nodding in approval, she blushed and proceeded towards the podium. However, as she stepped onto the podium, someone exclaimed, "Enter from outside! The teacher always enters from outside!" Responding quickly, Xiuxiu moved to the door and then returned to the podium to begin.

Just as she was about to commence the lesson, an unfortunate incident unfolded. Sanniu abruptly cautioned everyone, "We shouldn't have her as the teacher. Her father isn't reputable; he was dismissed a long time ago!"

The classroom fell silent all at once.

Xiuxiu was suddenly confronted with the seriousness of the situation. It wasn't just a playful exchange among classmates; her father had actually been dismissed. She had overheard her mother talking to Xingfen about his involvement in private trading and embezzlement, leaving the factory in significant debt. How had this news spread so rapidly? At that moment, she felt a sense of inferiority compared to her peers. Should she return to her seat and continue as a student, or should she hastily leave the classroom? Feeling the weight of everyone's gaze, she couldn't bear it any longer. Without a second thought, she dashed out of the classroom.

As Xiuxiu ran out, the classmates started to panic, but Sanniu shouted towards the door she just left, "No matter where she runs, her father won't be spared!"

Yuhu's actions went unnoticed as he quietly rose from his seat and remarked, "It's unfair to prevent Xiuxiu from being the teacher! Even though her father may not be exemplary, she still has a good mother!" Having said his piece, he settled back into his seat without uttering another word.

The classroom fell silent again.

At that moment, Xingfen suddenly walked in from outside.

The teacher's arrival injected a bit of vibrancy back into the classroom. Yet, Xingfen could sense that something had transpired in her absence. Assuming it must be due to her tardiness, she felt the need to address the matter. Scanning the classroom, she stated, "I typically don't condone tardiness, but today I'm the one who's late. I'm not exempt from the rules and owe you an apology. Now, let's proceed as planned and begin with phonetics."

When Xiuxiu rushed out of the classroom in a state of panic, she inadvertently left her school bag on the desk. So, who returned the bag to Xiuxiu after school? It was Yuhu, without a doubt. He always remembered what Xiuxiu had confided in him—that her father might not be kind, but she was fortunate to have a loving mother. It might have been this very reason that led to more bullying directed at her because of her father; the closer he tried to befriend her, the more some people ridiculed her. They would taunt, "Chirp chirp, cluck cluck, a big rooster followed by a little chick!" Yet, he paid no heed to their remarks.

Yuhu, shouldering his school bag, entered Xiuxiu's yard and overheard Xiuxiu's mother conversing with Xiuxiu inside the house. As he listened in, he discerned that they were discussing the recent incident at school.

Xiuxiu's mother remarked, "We shouldn't solely hold Sanniu responsible for this situation. It's because of your father! How are we going to manage? Now, Aunt Xingfen is also on the verge of departing. Going forward, you'll be staying at home to look after your younger sister."

As Xiuxiu's mother continued talking, she caught sight of Yuhu standing in the yard holding Xiuxiu's school bag. She hurriedly stepped out of the house to retrieve the bag from him, addressing him with an air of maturity, "If only Xiuxiu were more like you, that would be truly wonderful. Look at the state our family has come to."

Xiuxiu emerged from the house, standing beside her mother with a lowered gaze, unable to find any words to express herself. Yuhu, who had mulled over a few comforting words for Xiuxiu on his way there, now found himself unable to recall a single one.

Xiuxiu's mother, seemingly considering it natural for her daughter to face criticism occasionally, inquired about school and then shifted the conversation toward Xingfen's university plans.

As Yuhu prepared to depart, Xiuxiu escorted him to the door. Still unsure of what to say, he simply echoed the familiar words, "Xiuxiu, remember this. You have a good mother! My aunt said that when your dad rectifies his errors, he'll return to see you!" With that, he hurriedly left.

Upon hearing Yuhu's words, Xiuxiu felt a sense of relief wash over her. She lingered at the door for a moment before entering the house. Inside, she found her mother seated on the kang, rummaging through a bundle. The instant her mother began to flip through the contents of the bundle, Xiuxiu grasped exactly what she was about to do.

Xiuxiu's mother reflected on Xingfen, their neighbor and now Xiuxiu's teacher, who had always treated them with kindness despite the recent challenges involving Xiuxiu's father. With Xingfen's impending departure for university, she wanted to convey her appreciation. This had been a topic of discussion in their household for the past few days, and it was Xiuxiu who proposed the idea. Recognizing her mother's exceptional sewing skills—her hand-stitched seams were as precise as those done by a machine—Xiuxiu suggested creating a handmade backpack as a gift for Aunt Xingfen.

Having just received confirmation from Yuhu that Xingfen was preparing to sit for the university entrance exam, Xiuxiu's mother felt it was time to take action. She started rummaging through her bundles of fabrics.

Between old friends

As word spread about Xingfen's upcoming schooling, not only did the adults plan to give gifts to express their gratitude, but even the children in the preschool had their own ideas brewing. As the news circulated further, everyone began formulating their individual plans.

This morning, once Sanniu, accompanied by Xiaozhu and Erxing, had completed their breakfast, they quietly departed from the village along the perimetre wall. Upon reaching the village entrance, Xiaozhu and Erxing each passed a handful of coins to Sanniu. Thereafter, they dashed eagerly towards the town.

It was early summer now, and once the three of them departed from the village, they swiftly removed their shirts, baring their torsos to the warmth of the sun. Sanniu, a seasoned member of the "Gorillas", demonstrated both speed and agility, deftly navigating shortcuts and weaving through the dense cornfields, leading the way. Xiaozhu and Erxing closely trailed behind, maintaining a respectable distance. By the time the sun reached its zenith in the sky, they had reached the thoroughfare of the town. Sanniu guided them from East Street to West Street, and then from South Street to North Street.

Though Sanniu commenced his schooling tardily, he exhibited rapidity in rectifying his errors. Particularly with Xingfen commending his recent advancements, Sanniu found himself more inclined towards enhancement. Only a few days prior, he frequently employed coarse language, yet presently, he had nearly forsaken it altogether. Consequently, he harbored a desire to convey his appreciation to Miss Zhang. Today, accompanied by Xiaozhu and Erxing, Sanniu embarks on an excursion to the town to procure gifts for Xingfen.

On the town's streets, an array of shops

stood side by side. Sanniu took the lead into a stationery shop. The trio leaned against the counter, scanning the merchandise from end to end. Eventually, Sanniu halted before the notebooks. He wiped the sweat from his brow, glanced at the prices labeled on the notebooks, and tallied the coins in his pocket. Eventually, he gestured towards a notebook that wasn't the smallest and said, "I'll have this one, please."

Taking out the notebook, the salesperson accepted his money and gave him the change.

In the afternoon, when Yuhu was heading to school, he ran into Sanniu and Xiaozhu at the school gate. He spoke to them bluntly, "Are you still students or not?"

Xiaozhu puffed out his chest and said, "Yes, we are!"

"Then why do you skip school?"

"We had something to do," Xiaozhu

replied.

Seeing that Xiaozhu was about to reveal their secret, Sanniu tugged on his clothes and stepped forward to say to Yuhu, "Go home and take a look. You'll find out when you are in the small room at the west of your yard."

With that, the two of them dashed into the classroom.

After school, recalling Sanniu's advice, Yuhu returned home and immediately opened the door to the small room. Suddenly, he noticed a line of small paper parcels neatly arranged on the kang, each labeled "To Miss Zhang".

Out of curiosity, Yuhu unwrapped one of the paper parcels, discovering two pencils within; proceeding to another, he found it filled with a handful of red dates. Upon opening yet another, the contents proved even more intriguing—a Sun Wukong (a prominent character from the classic Chinese novel *Journey to the West*), crafted from cardboard with limbs that could be manipulated.

Eventually, he unveiled another paper parcel, revealing a small green notebook. This was the item that Sanniu and the others had procured from the stationery emporium in town. Yuhu turned to the first page and found a few unevenly drawn pencil characters inscribed upon it:

To: Student Xingfen
　　By Wang Erniu, Li Xiaozhu, Wang
　　　　　　　　　　Erxing

Yuhu suddenly grasped the situation. Sanniu and the other two had skipped school in the morning to purchase this small green notebook. He glanced at the other paper parcels, considering that they might also be gifts from Sanniu. He muttered to himself, "Why do I always dwell on Sanniu's faults? Can't I focus on his improvements instead?"

Yuhu's grandma called Yuhu from the yard to have dinner, but Yuhu was so lost in his thoughts that he forgot to respond.

After dinner, Yuhu, under the moonlight, ran straight to Sanniu's house and called out into the yard, "Sanniu, come out for a moment!"

Sanniu initially thought the voice sounded like Yuhu's, but then he dismissed the idea. It couldn't be Yuhu. While they used to be friends, ever since Yuhu began smoking, he had distanced himself and never joined Sanniu in any activities.

Yuhu beckoned for Sanniu once more.

This time, Sanniu was certain it was for him. He pondered if the class prefect is seeking me out, it must be either due to an error I've made or because they're dissatisfied with the gift I presented. Suddenly, he recollected the altercation with Xiuxiu during yesterday's lesson. Well, it's his responsibility, and he ought to acknowledge it. With that in mind, he emerged from the house into the courtyard.

Sure enough, it was Yuhu standing in the yard. Sanniu summoned his courage and advanced, purposefully avoiding any mention of the gift. He stated, "Yuhu, I am aware of my error, and I assure you, I will rectify it."

Yuhu didn't speak.

"I will correct," Sanniu said again. "If Lin Xiuxiu wasn't a girl, I would have gone to apologise to her alone a long time ago. How about you taking me to apologise to her?"

Sanniu's conversation was veering off-topic, yet Yuhu sensed a growing closeness between them. He approached Sanniu with his hands held behind his back and asked, "Sanniu, are you still up for making a promise with me by sealing it with a pinky swear?"

Sanniu was confused. He couldn't figure out what was going on. He quickly asked Yuhu, "What did you say?"

"A pinky swear!" Yuhu said.

"With me?"

"Yes, it's you." As Yuhu spoke, he also reached out his hand to Sanniu.

Now Sanniu understood what was going on. He hastily wiped his right hand on his pants and reached out it to Yuhu.

Under the moonlight, their fingers were finally hooked together.

After Yuhu and Sanniu had made their

promise, Yuhu really led Sanniu to Xiuxiu's house.

Xiuxiu's mother presented a new school bag, urging Xiuxiu to swiftly deliver it to Xingfen. Upon inspecting the bag, she noticed two peony flowers adorning it. Set against the verdant fabric, the blooms appeared remarkably lifelike, almost exuding a scent. Yet, they were neither embroidered nor painted. How were they fashioned? Xiuxiu's mother gently probed and examined them, realizing they were crafted from cloth. She carried them beneath the electric light for a closer examination, observing the flowers' edges adorned with red thread, boasting stitches of various sizes. Besides Xiuxiu, who else possessed such skill?

At that moment, Yuhu entered first, with Sanniu trailing behind. Both of them displayed a hint of shyness. Yuhu addressed her as "Auntie" in greeting, and Sanniu followed suit, albeit softly. Sanniu's voice was notably subdued compared to his usual tone, but both Xiuxiu's mother and Xiuxiu heard it distinctly.

"Go ahead and say it," Yuhu urged Sanniu, stepping aside.

"You, you do it for me!" Sanniu blushed for the first time.

Upon hearing this, Xiuxiu's mother understood what was going on. She called them over and said, "Forget about it. Just take a look at the school bag I just made."

Yuhu and Sanniu immediately noticed the peony flowers on the school bag.

"Look at these flowers. They're just like real ones," Yuhu said.

"The flowers were stitched by Xiuxiu,"

Xiuxiu's mother affirmed, sensing a familiarity in their appearance. Suddenly, her heart skipped a beat. Setting down the school bag, she made her way to the kang, retrieving Xiuxiu's expansive quilt adorned with flower patterns, and unfurled it. True to her suspicion, there were two gaps precisely where the flowers should have been.

Xiuxiu's mother was angry.

Observing the shift in Xiuxiu's mother's expression, Sanniu promptly positioned himself in front of Xiuxiu and remarked, "My sister has some floral fabric. It even features large peonies. I'll fetch you a piece to mend the quilt! I'm confident I can procure it!"

Normally, even if Xiuxiu's mother were in good spirits, she wouldn't overlook such a matter. However, today was an exception. She erupted into laughter and remarked, "You needn't fret about it. Deliver the school bag to Xingfen. I'll mend the quilt when I find the time."

The bell tolls on the red roof

This summer, Zhang Village celebrates two joyous occasions: firstly, the kindergarten's new abode boasting red walls and roofs; secondly, the impending commencement of the academic pursuits of students who have secured admission to universities and secondary vocational schools.

The decision to renovate the school just as the kindergarten students were preparing to graduate likely stemmed from the dismissal of Big Horse Face from his position. Subsequently, prior to Grandpa Wugeng and Aunt Xingfen attempting to contact the brick and tile factory, the factory took the initiative to supply two trucks of red tiles. A car, sounding its horn, pulled up to the school gate, and an individual emerged from the vehicle—revealing themselves to be the factory director. Upon learning of the situation, he personally participated in the delivery of the tiles. Some questioned the rationale behind installing a red roof when the children were on the cusp of graduating. Both Grandpa Wugeng and the factory director responded in unison, asserting that while the current children may soon move on, there would always be new ones, and as they grow, there will inevitably be more to follow.

Soon after, the preschool truly transformed into a red-roofed building.

Grandpa Wugeng, drawing inspiration

from the town's middle school, constructed a smaller red-roofed structure atop the grand red roof, wherein he installed a sizable bell. With a firm grip, Grandpa Wugeng tugged on the rope, causing the bell to chime melodiously. "This is a more refined approach than blowing a whistle!" he remarked, nodding in satisfaction.

Recent news arrived concerning the university students' enrollment. Notifications came from Beijing, Tianjin, and Baoding. Grandpa Wugeng personally delivered the admission letters to the university students.

Today marks the departure of the university students, an occasion of unparalleled joy in Zhang Village after many years. In previous times, when students received recommendations for university, news of their departure often arrived after they had already left, making it impossible to bid them farewell. Thus, Grandpa Wugeng took to the loudspeaker early this morning to announce, "Attention all commune members! Attention all commune members! Please assemble in front of the red-roofed house this morning to bid farewell to our university students. The more, the merrier!"

As soon as Grandpa Wugeng finished, people lined up in front of the red house, forming a row that stretched down the entire street.

There were Yuhu's grandfather, Grandma Wubao, Xiaozhu's parents, Xiaorong's parents, Erxing's elder brother, Meihua's sister, Qinglin's aunt, Sanniu's uncle, and Xiuxiu's mother. Even Qiaozhen stood at a distance.

The parents of the new university students stood at the very front. The Youth League had already prepared several large red flowers and placed one on each of them.

Now, Yuhu led the kindergarten students forward, with San Niu at the vanguard, clutching a small flag. Yuhu barked out orders as they proceeded in a disciplined manner. Observing the procession, Grandma Wubao remarked to Yuhu's grandfather, "Only recently, they were causing mischief in the streets. Yet, look at them now, marching so orderly."

In no time, Grandpa Wugeng arrived with the new university students, Uncle Gao Xing, and the secondary vocational students, Sister Caiyun and Auntie Xiaoxia. Some might have expected Xingfen to be among them, but she was absent.

Where's Xingfen? Ah, there she is, approaching with the gifts bestowed upon her by the students the other day cradled in her arms. Is Xingfen truly taking the gifts with her to university? You would be mistaken. Xingfen is actually on her way to present the gifts to Uncle Gao and the others. So, is Xingfen not embarking on her university journey? This time, you've guessed correctly. But why isn't Xingfen attending university? Grandpa Wugeng will soon enlighten us.

Xingfen approached the three new students and presented a small green notebook to Uncle Gao, remarking, "Gao Xing, this is for you. Let's see if it suits your fancy."

Gaoxing reached for the notebook, intending to stow it in his pocket. However, Xingfen interjected, "Hold on, don't conceal it just yet. There are words inside. Read them first." With that, Gaoxing opened the notebook and perused the inscription:

"University Student Li Gaoxing's Homework Notebook. Presented by Wang Sanniu, Li Xiaozhu, and Wang Erxing." Needless to say, Xingfen had altered the names on the cover. After reading, Gaoxing was overcome with joy, rendered speechless by the gesture.

Xingfen proceeded to approach Caiyun and Xiaoxia, presenting them with their respective gifts. In the midst of this, Xiuxiu, amidst the crowd, observed that the only item remaining in Xingfen's possession was the school bag adorned with peony flowers. Xiuxiu harbored a reluctance to see Miss Zhang give it to anyone else. Despite acknowledging the prestigious honor of being a university student, she felt a reluctance to part with it to others.

Xingfen appeared to have anticipated Xiuxiu's desires. When someone inquired,

"Who will receive the flower-patterned school bag?" Xingfen whimsically swung the bag and declared, "This is my treasure, and I shan't part with it for anyone!" With that, she joined the line of students.

Now it was Grandpa Wugeng's moment to address the gathering. Speaking in an unaffected manner, he conversed as if discussing everyday affairs, "I had the confidence that our Zhang Village would nurture some exceptional talents this time around. You see, don't you? It's quite an achievement! If it weren't for everyone's shared aspirations towards the Four Modernizations, we wouldn't have reached this milestone today!"

"But don't think yourselves superior just because you've entered university or vocational school. What about those who didn't sit the university entrance exam? Look," Grandpa Wugeng gestured towards Xingfen, "she's chosen to remain in the village for the betterment of these children's education. While others pursue exams, she dedicates herself to aiding them, sacrificing her own rest and comfort. Isn't that a mark of success? Xingfen possesses foresight. In a decade or more, who can say how many university students, scientists, and intellectuals will emerge from this crimson building? That's the essence of it!"

After Grandpa Wugeng concluded his address, he cast a glance at Auntie Xingfen, indicating that she too should step forward and share a few words to convey her sentiments. However, Xingfen diverted her attention to the line of students and declared, "Yuhu, sing us a song!"

After speaking that, she noticed that Yuhu was not in the line. Instead, the sound of a bell rang from the red roof.

As the bell tolled, all eyes turned towards the red house. They beheld the sizable bell suspended beneath the modest red roof, swaying to and fro as it chimed, almost as if it were serenading and greeting each onlooker with a wave.

Someone in the crowd shouted, "It's Yuhu ringing the bell!"

Writer's Album

Photo of the self-written and self-performed play *The Ideal* during her high school period. The writer Tie Ning is the first from right to left in the back row.

The 1980s. She wrote the short story *Ah, Xiangxue*.

1985. She attended the National Short Story Awards Ceremony in Nanjing, China, and her novella *The Red Shirt Without Buttons* and short story *June's Big Topic* both won awards.

The late 1980s. Her novel *Rose Door* was just published.

Autumn, 1990. She was picking radishes in the remote mountains of Laishui County, Hebei Province, China.

1991. She was visiting Bing Xin.

1995. She was at an elementary school in the United States.

The 1990s. She was at a primary school in the mountainous areas of Hebei Province, China.

2005. During the "Revisiting the Long March, hailing the New Era" event organized by the China Writers Association, she was with students from Aba Tibetan School in Sichuan Province, China.

May 2009. At the China Writers Association's "Talent Development Library Project" award ceremony, she was with students from a deaf-mute school.

June 2011. She was in the dormitory for students from Tu ethnic minority in the Third Middle School of Huzhu Tu Autonomous County, Xining City, Qinghai Province, China.

July 2011. She was visiting the centenarian Yang Jiang.

May 2016. In Xiji County, Ningxia Hui Autonomous Region, she was with students after giving the first lecture of "Literature Illuminates Life" public lecture series organized by the China Writers Association.

July 2018. She observed art volunteer teachers guiding local students performing the Gaoshan Opera at Binhe Middle School, Wudu District, Longnan City, Gansu Province, China.

May 2019. She participated in a reading salon at 8 p.m. held by Naiman Baner Cultural Centre during a research visit to Naiman Banner, Tongliao City, Inner Mongolia Autonomous Region, China.

July 2019. She was in Xiangxi Tujiazu&Miaozu Autonomous Prefecture, Hunan Province, China.

October 2019. She participated in a Chinese dance performance event in Mauritius with Shanti Bai Hanoomanjee, the speaker of the National Assembly of Mauritius, and others.

Writer's Handwriting

我在北京的胡同里住过，我曾经也是北京胡同里的一个女孩子。胡同里那群快乐的、多话的、有点缺心少肺的女孩子我一直玩着。我常常觉得，要是没了她们，胡同还能叫胡同吗？还嗯，如今的北京，已不再是从前，她不再那么既矜持又恬淡、既清高又随和了。她学会了拥抱，她怀里全注着多少北京之外的人啊。胡同里那些带点咬舌音的、嘎嘣利落脆的贫北京话也早就不受戴见了——从前的那些女孩子，她们就是说着一口贫北京话也活在胡同里的。她们神情大方，小心眼儿不多，叫人觉得随财都可能受骗。二十多年过去了，

www.ingramcontent.com/pod-product-compliance
Lightning Source LLC
Chambersburg PA
CBHW041751010726
47507CB00009B/352